D0396870

The WISDOM *of the* SHIRE

ALSO BY NOBLE SMITH

Stolen from Gypsies

Sparks in the Park

✴ The WISDOM of the SHIRE

———•———

A SHORT GUIDE TO
A LONG AND HAPPY LIFE

NOBLE SMITH

FOREWORD BY PETER S. BEAGLE

THOMAS DUNNE BOOKS
St. Martin's Press 📖 New York

THOMAS DUNNE BOOKS.
An imprint of St. Martin's Press.

THE WISDOM OF THE SHIRE. Copyright © 2012 by Noble Smith. Foreword copyright © 2012 by Peter S. Beagle. All rights reserved. Printed in the United States of America. For information, address St. Martin's Press, 175 Fifth Avenue, New York, N.Y. 10010.

www.thomasdunnebooks.com
www.stmartins.com

Design by Kelly S. Too

ISBN 978-1-250-02556-2 (hardcover)
ISBN 978-1-250-02641-5 (e-book)

First Edition: November 2012

10 9 8 7 6 5 4 3 2 1

For my dad, who didn't understand Hobbits,
and then mysteriously became one

CONTENTS

FOREWORD

The Wisdom of the Shire is an idea whose time has unquestionably come. In an age awash in self-help books and loosely "spiritual" guides to living a truly fulfilled human life, it's hard to believe that no one thought of taking J.R.R. Tolkien's Hobbits—the Little-folk, the Halflings— as examples, both physical and philosophical, of just such a life. Especially with the release of Peter Jackson's film trilogy of *The Hobbit*, Noble Smith's book is bound to create a unique niche for itself, and an audience certainly not limited solely to Tolkien devotees.

As a presumed expert on the writings of J.R.R. Tolkien (I still receive occasional letters in calligraphed Elvish), the scenarist of the animated version of *The Lord of the Rings* and one whose own work is frequently—and erroneously—bracketed with his, I have felt myself to be Tolkiened-out for a long time.

Yet reading Noble Smith's book made me want to re-read *The Hobbit* and *The Lord of the Rings* immediately, and to reconsider the earthy, generous, joyously sensual lives of the beings with whom their author, by his own account, most truly identified. *The Wisdom of the Shire* reminds the reader that our world isn't—or doesn't have to be—all that removed from Middle-earth, the Shire and the Party Tree. I'd buy it like a shot, give copies away to deserving friends and keep it by the bed for bad nights.

—PETER S. BEAGLE

I am in fact a *Hobbit* (in all but size). I like gardens, trees and unmechanized farmlands; I smoke a pipe, and like good plain food . . . I go to bed late and get up late (when possible).

—J.R.R. Tolkien (excerpted from
The Letters of J.R.R. Tolkien, #213)

The fire's very cosy here, and the food's good. What more could one want?

—Bilbo talking about Rivendell
from *The Return of the King*

The WISDOM of the SHIRE

*

INTRODUCTION

I discovered J.R.R. Tolkien when I was a Hobbit. Actually, I was a twelve-year-old boy and very short for my age, longing for adventure. Hobbit*ish*, one might say. Like so many millions of other readers I fell into Middle-earth as though I'd tumbled through a portal into an alternate reality—a reality I did not want to leave.

I raced through the Tolkien canon with the speed of Gandalf's horse Shadowfax, thrilling at *The Hobbit*, devouring *The Lord of the Rings* and mining every last detail of *The Silmarillion*. When Peter Jackson's movies came out decades later I was overjoyed by the passion that went into the films. The filmmakers revered the books just as much as the rest of us.

Throughout my life I've never gotten over that sense of happy surprise at discovering someone else who loves

Tolkien. I've seen his books on the shelves of famous play-wrights and industrious farmers, successful businesspeople and cutting edge computer scientists. All of these men and women shared something in common: they loved the Hob-bits more than anyone else in Tolkien's tales.

That's because there's something about the *character* of the Hobbits (and not the characters *called* Hobbits) that makes them live inside us in a profound and lasting way. Tolkien crafted Middle-earth in his mind, but the Hobbits sprang from his heart. Our lives might be better if some of the traits of these cheerful, honest, steadfast and industrious people could become our own.

And that's what I've set out to do in this book. To show how the habits of the Hobbits and the wisdom of the Shire can be relevant to those of us residing *outside* of Middle-earth. Tolkien's heroes might be works of fiction, but the lessons we can take from their adventures are wonderfully real and meaningful to our lives.

✳

WHERE IS THE SHIRE?

I like to believe Tolkien was the first alternate reality historian. Middle-earth was just as real to Professor Tolkien as the country in which he lived. In his imagination he'd walked all over the hills and woodlands of the Shire, and sat in front of the blazing fireplace at Rivendell, and even climbed the dizzying stairs of Cirith Ungol. He'd visited all of these places in his mind and then he wrote about them with a clarity few authors have rivaled.✱

Middle-earth was all in his head. But thankfully, now it's in our heads too.

Even though early Medieval England is not the setting for the Shire, many of the place-names come

✱ From the years 1930 to 1947 J.R.R. Tolkien and his family lived at 20 Northmoor Road, Oxford. It was in the drawing room of this house that Tolkien wrote *The Hobbit* and nearly all of *The Lord of the Rings*.

✳ The Shire is divided up into four parts called "farthings" (another Old English word) consisting of East, West, North and Southfarthing. Hobbiton is in the Westfarthing.

✳ Buckland, where the famous Brandybuck family hails from, is like a tiny sovereign nation and is not "officially" part of the Shire. It lies on the eastern edge of the Shire and is bordered by the River Brandywine on one side, and the Old Forest on the other.

from the Anglo-Saxon era. The word "shire" itself, for example, is Old English for "county."✳

The Shire is eighteen thousand square miles—about the size of the states of Vermont and New Hampshire put together. The United Kingdom, by comparison, is five times that size. Hobbiton, where Bag End is located, is situated almost exactly in the center of the Shire.✳

When the Hobbits first settled their little country, around thirteen hundred years before Bilbo Baggins was born, they became instantly attached to the land and developed what Tolkien called "a close friendship with the earth." It's a beautiful way of saying they are as much a part of the Shire as the soil, stones, rivers and trees.

Chapter 1

HOW SNUG IS YOUR
HOBBIT-HOLE?

Throughout my life I've often heard people describe a snug home or a particularly cozy room as being "just like a Hobbit-hole." This is one of the highest compliments a Tolkien fan can give, for it's the sort of place where they'd want to spend some serious leisure time—to read a book or have a conversation, to eat a delicious meal or just sit and think.

On the very first page of *The Hobbit* Tolkien introduced the world to Bilbo Baggins (and Middle-earth for that matter) with a lengthy and loving description of a Hobbit-hole. His Halflings are, without a doubt, creatures of comfort. But they don't live in ostentatious mansions or castles of stone. Their cozy homes, built into the sides of hills for optimal insulation, are cheery wood-paneled refuges with fireplaces, well-stocked pantries, featherbeds and pretty

* In some parts of ancient Britain, Neolithic people lived in crude underground homes called "pit houses" dug into the sides of hills. These may have been the inspiration for Tolkien's Hobbit-holes.

* Drogo Baggins was Frodo's father. He and Frodo's mother Primula died in a boating accident.

gardens right outside their deep-set windows.*

Peter Jackson's film adaptations show Bag End in all its oak paneled and glowing hearth fire glory. Who wouldn't want to inhabit that welcoming house with its hand-hewn beams, big round front door and cozy sun-dappled kitchen? The fact that you're reading this book means you're most likely smiling wistfully right now thinking, *I would live there faster than you can say "Drogo Baggins's boat!"**

In *The Hobbit*, when Bilbo is trapped inside the Elven-king's palace—existing as an invisible and lonely thief without a bed to call his own—he wishes he were back in his dear home, sitting by the fireplace with a shining lamp on his table. To him this is the height of comfort. Warmth. Light. Peace of mind. We must remember that Bilbo rushed out of his home in such a hurry to join Thorin Oakenshield and his band of Dwarves that he'd forgotten to bring a pocket-handkerchief!

When I was a boy I tried to turn my drab suburban bedroom into my own private Hobbit-hole. I found an old wingback chair at the local thrift shop—a chair suitable for marathon sessions of *The Lord of the Rings*. I stacked my shelves with Tolkien books I'd rescued from used-bookstores. I started a secondhand pipe collection (assuring my mom they were "Just for show!") and bought some cheap drugstore pipe tobacco called "Borkum Riff," placing it in a big jar I labeled Longbottom Leaf. Every time I opened the lid it filled my room with a scent redolent (at least I thought) of Bag End. This room was my refuge, even though it probably reeked like the back of a union hall.

Over the years I've found I was not alone in my earnest longing for a Hobbit-hole to call my own. This notion, however absurd, appeals to many of us Shire enthusiasts. Some people have managed to create their own versions of Bag End, like Simon Dale in the United Kingdom who built an abode worthy of Hobbiton. The house, half-buried in the Welsh countryside, was entirely fashioned by hand out of local materials such as stones and wood from surrounding forests. It has a roof that collects water for the garden and an air-cooled fridge.✳

There are very few places throughout the various Half-flings' adventures that offer a facsimile of the extreme comforts of the Shire home: the magical Rivendell with

✳ Simon Dale is building a new house as part of the Lammas Project, a low-impact ecovillage in Pembrokeshire, Wales. It's a sustainable community where the residents grow their own food, pool resources and build homes from materials at hand, very much like in the Shire of Middle-earth. You can learn more at lammas.org.uk.

its whispering trees, soft beds, wistful Elves and Lays of the Elder Days Poetry Nights; Tom Bombadil's cottage nestled in the woods near the gurgling Withywindle River, complete with chef Goldberry—ravishing daughter of the River-king; and Beorn's wooden hall with its endless supply of honey cakes, mead and waitstaff of trained bipedal animals.

All of these locations have something in common, despite their curious inhabitants. Like Hobbit-holes they're safe, warm, comfortable and filled with good food. They're homey places to rest and regenerate before a long journey, and they're connected to the natural world in a way that makes them almost part of the surroundings.

Modern homes are a sharp contrast to the cheery Hobbit-holes and have become repositories for cheap imported junk that we toss out like so much rubbish after a few short years of use. For many of us our connection to the world outside our homes is what we see from our cars in bumper-to-bumper traffic on the way to hermetically sealed office buildings. Urban sprawl or "Orc-ification"* is turning our cities and towns into vast and ugly corporate retail outlets.

Everything inside and outside a Hobbit-hole would have been made by hand. And it would all have been created to last a lifetime, from the brass knob in the center of the big round front door, to the clay mugs in the kitchen, to the chair

---

* The word "Orc" comes from the Old English for "hell-demon."

in front of the fire. When did we all become so helpless that we stopped learning how to make or fix the simplest things? Why don't we expect the same sort of permanence and quality in our own lives?

There are ways to change. Internet sites like Makezine .com show people all over the globe making remarkable utilitarian objects by hand, and Instructables.com will teach you the step-by-step process of how to build and mend things you would have thought were impossible. Online retailers like Etsy allow hundreds of thousands of craftspeople from all across the world to sell their handmade items (everything from furniture to clothes to ironmongery) to millions of buyers. These artisans are making amazing things out of recycled products as well as upcycled materials.✶

Seventy years ago Tolkien lamented how machines seemed to be taking over the world. Everywhere he looked trees were being cut down to make way for ugly garages, gasworks and factories. (Imagine how he would feel about the state of things now.) He wrote most of *The Lord of the Rings* during WWII at his house in Oxford while thunderous warplanes roared overhead flying off to Europe. He mused grimly that Moloch must have taken over as ruler of the world.✶

✶ Upcycling: the process of converting waste products or useless materials into something of greater value and benefit to the environment.

✶ Moloch: an ancient god who could only be appeased through child sacrifice.

Tolkien wrote often to his son Christopher (his chief audience for his stories) who was serving in the Royal Air Force at the time, sending him chapters of *The Lord of the Rings* as soon as he could get copies typed up. In his letters he described to his son the little joys of life back in Oxford. He also told him about the simple trials and tribulations of being a homeowner. Reading about the mundane, when you're far from home, is sometimes just as interesting as hearing about the sublime.✴

Tolkien had seen the horrors of mechanized war firsthand, having served in the trenches of WWI in France. Like the Hobbits in *The Lord of the Rings*, he'd returned from the desolation of the battlefield to a changed world— a world where all but one of his friends no longer walked the Earth. Ten years after the Great War he was staring at a blank page of paper when the opening lines of *The Hobbit* popped into his head.

And thus was born the first Hobbit—the reluctant hero who departs his beloved abode and returns from a great adventure a changed man. We'd all be lucky in life if we had the chance to experience an unexpected adventure, and then make our way back

---

✴ Tolkien's house had originally been designed for Basil Blackwell, owner of Oxford's most famous bookstore and publishing house. B.H. Blackwell Publishing gave Tolkien his first break in 1915 by including his poem "Goblin Feet" in an anthology called *Oxford Poetry*. At the time Tolkien was only twenty-three years old.

safely to a place of comfort. Sometimes the only way we can appreciate our home and the simple happiness it has to offer is to be away from it for a while.

After the battle of the Pelennor Fields, when Merry is recovering in Gondor's Houses of Healing from his brave attack on the dread Witch-king of Angmar, he tells Pippin that one thing alone has sustained him through the hardships of his terrible journey: the deep spiritual roots he's put down in his beloved Shire.

This is Merry's Hobbit-hole of the mind.

Try to think of a place in your own life that was like a Hobbit-hole. It could have been your beloved grandparents' living room, or a kindly music teacher's studio or a good friend's comfy apartment. What was it about that place that made you feel at home? That allowed you to dream? Was it the space itself, or the people in it? Or a combination of both? At some point in your life your subconscious put down "roots" in this place, and you can take strength from this memory, even if the actual place no longer exists.

You can create a snug "Hobbit-hole" wherever you are—in your office, in a hotel room, in a college dormitory, in an apartment in the city or a bedroom in the suburbs. Because the space which you inhabit is irrelevant compared to the power of your mind to project contentment. For me that contentment has always meant having a good book at hand, so that no matter where I was stuck physically, my mind was free to soar.

* The span of time between the beginning of *The Hobbit* and the end of *The Lord of the Rings* is exactly eighty years.

In the final scene of *The Lord of the Rings,* Sam Gamgee returns from the Grey Havens to Bag End, arriving at night. He's just said good-bye to Frodo forever and he is terribly sad. But then he sees the cheery yellow glow of firelight emanating from the house that now belongs to him—a home bequeathed to him by Frodo. The house itself—the structure—is not important, however. It's what's inside: his loving wife and daughter waiting for him with a warm meal on the table.

It's a beautiful bookend to Tolkien's beloved novels: *The Hobbit* starts at Bag End with a callow bachelor and *The Lord of the Rings* ends there with a wise father. All of Tolkien's great adventures are set in between the opening and closing of the door to a simple and yet miraculous dwelling called a Hobbit-hole.*

the wisdom of the shire tells us . . .

"Your true home is inside your heart and stays with you wherever you go; but a nice snug room is a lovely thing to come back home to!"

Chapter 2

EAT LIKE A BRANDYBUCK,
DRINK LIKE A TOOK

Hobbits are quite possibly the most lovable foodies* in all of literature. They are constantly astounding Elves and Men and even Dwarves (who are voracious eaters and drinkers in their own rights) with their fathomless stomachs and thirsty throats. They eat six meals a day, as Tolkien tells us in the prologue to *The Lord of the Rings*, at least "when they could get them."

Bread and cheese, butter and clotted cream, mushrooms, sausages and rashers of bacon . . . and beer. Quarts and quarts of beer. These are the staples of Hobbits who will pester and scrounge to fill their growling bellies.

Meriadoc Brandybuck and Peregrin Took (aka Merry and Pippin) are the finest examples of Hobbit epicureanism. After the colossal

* Foodies: aficionados of food and drink.

Battle of Isengard—where the army of tree-like giant Ents destroys the evil wizard Saruman's high walls—the rascally pair raid the sorcerer's storerooms for provisions and stuff themselves silly on rashers of bacon, salted-pork, bread and honey. Aragorn, Gimli and Legolas find them lounging atop the ruined walls, smoking their pipes contentedly. What's the first thing Merry and Pippin do? They join their friends in a *second* luncheon!

When Gandalf whisks poor Pippin away to the citadel of Minas Tirith, the Hobbit's first urgent questions upon arrival are, "Where are the dining rooms? The inns? And where can he get a decent draught of beer?" Who cares if the undead Lord of the Nazgûl and his raving gang of Ringwraiths are trying to hunt him down like a Buckland rat. All he's been thinking about on the long ride from Isengard is bread and ale, the poor ravenous little chap!

In *The Hobbit* Bilbo's growling stomach is a persistent reminder of the vast and adored pantries he's left behind at his home in Bag End. He's like having a grumpy ten-year-old boy along for a cross-country car trip who is constantly complaining about being hungry.

What was so appealing to the Hobbits about food from the Shire? It's the most basic kind of fare, after all. But sometimes the simplest things done up the right way are the most delicious. When was the last time you had a slice of homemade bread with homemade jam? I promise you it is one of the most scrumptious (to use Gollum's favorite word) things to eat in Middle-earth or *this* Earth. Everything we eat now is processed and watered down and concocted to trick us with "natural flavors." We've lost our taste for what is real and honest and, well, Hobbitish. When we dine on fast food, we might as well be eating Orc food.✳

✳ What did Orcs eat? Man-flesh and other Orcs! When marching they drank a thick dark alcohol to give them vigor. They forced this down Merry's and Pippin's throats and it filled them with a "fiery glow." It was Orc energy drink!

Tolkien said he identified with the Hobbits more than any other characters in his works. So why was Tolkien so obsessed with eating? Perhaps the nightmarish months he spent in the barren wastelands of the trenches during WWI (about as close as our world has ever gotten to Sauron's desolation of Mordor) made him keenly aware of the value and beauty of good food. Like the other soldiers at the front, he would have existed on the few ounces of bread and cheese and boiled vegetables allotted daily. He spent several long months recovering from trench fever in a hospital back in England where patients were served reviving meals like the delightful sounding "toast water" and the oh so mouthwatering "jellied beef tea custard."

Or maybe it was the food shortages that occurred during WWII (while Tolkien was writing much of *The Lord of the Rings*) when butter and bacon were rationed and an adult was allowed a single egg for an entire week. Tea, a

* While Tolkien was a professor at Oxford one of his favorite hangouts was the pub called The Eagle and Child (known to locals as "The Bird and the Baby"). Here his group of writer friends known as *The Inklings* (along with the creator of the *Narnia* books C. S. Lewis) would have lunch and a few pints and discuss the stories they were writing.

favorite of Hobbits, continued to be rationed until 1952, two years before *The Fellowship of the Ring* was published.

Whatever the reason, Tolkien had his Hobbits turn to food for comfort in nearly every situation.* In their long and weary journey through the land of Mordor, Sam Gamgee wistfully reminisces about fish and chips, much to the disgust of the nearly cannibalistic Gollum who is used to eating fish (and smallish goblins) in the raw. "Keep your chips," sneers Gollum, to which Sam replies in disgust, "Oh, you're hopeless!"

Sam, however, cannot stop thinking of a homely meal, "something hot out of the pot" with "taters and carrots." Shire food is a reminder of happier times. Of civilization and goodness. When Gollum catches some rabbits for them to eat, Sam manages to find herbs for a stew—herbs nosed out in a strange war-torn land! (Now that's an undaunted Hobbit chef.)

A Hobbit like Sam would have spent his entire life eating everything from within an area fifty miles in diameter surrounding Hobbiton. Is it possible to survive like this in our modern age? The answer is an emphatic "yes," and people are doing it all over the world. It's called being a *locavore.** Give it a try. See how much food you

* Locavore: a person interested in eating foods that are locally grown and produced.

can discover to eat that's produced within a hundred miles or so of where you live. Nowadays, the average food item on our grocery store shelves travels up to fifteen hundred miles before it gets there. That's just about the distance from Hobbiton to Mount Doom.

Shop at your local farmers market and meet the people who are growing organic food in your area—food that hasn't been genetically modified or shipped across the ocean in a bulk freighter. Small farmers (they work on tiny *farms* and are not, as a rule, tiny *people*) are a lot like real-life industrious Hobbits, and entering a farmers market feels as if you're stepping back in time to another age when people knew who grew their food, and the land where they grew it.

Or try foraging for food in the wild like a Hobbit. Mushrooms, we're told, made the Shire-folk greedier than anything. When Frodo was a lad he'd risked being attacked by Farmer Maggot's vicious dogs (named Grip, Fang and Wolf) just to steal some of the delicious fungi off his land. Anyone who has ever hunted for the elusive and succulent morels knows the allure that mushroom

✱ You can read: *Edible Wild Plants* by John Kallas.

✱ In Southampton, England, is a pub called The Hobbit where you can get drinks with names like "The Frodo" (double vodka, peach schnapps, cranberry juice, lemonade) and sing your favorite Elvish lay at "Tom Bombadil's Cabaret Open Mic Night."

hunting can have when it takes hold. Aragorn was a great forager and tells the Hobbits they won't starve in the wilderness with him guiding them because he can find "berry, root and herb."

Foraging has become a popular pastime and there are many resources (in books and on the Internet) explaining where it's legal on public lands to harvest mushrooms or berries. Blackberries grow almost everywhere and you can easily preserve them for a taste of summer in the wintertime. Or try a local U-pick blueberry farm—the kind where they let you eat as much as you like while you're filling your buckets. Kids (most of whom eat like Hobbits) will love this too.✱

The very first time we meet Hobbits in *The Lord of the Rings* they're introduced as a sort of Greek chorus sitting around a table at an inn called The Ivy Bush, drinking ale and discussing the party preparations for Mr. Bilbo Baggins's eleventy-first birthday and gossiping about the strange goings-on in the world outside the Shire. The Hobbits love a good pub (or inn as they're referred to in Middle-earth).✱ The Golden Perch is a famous inn of

Buckland, and both Sam and Pippin are distraught when they can't partake of its renowned drink, thwarted in their quest to taste "the best beer in the Eastfarthing" by those pesky screeching Ringwraiths who are hot on their hairy heels.

The movie version of *The Fellowship of the Ring* captured the Hobbits' beery glee perfectly in the scene at The Prancing Pony in Bree where Merry brings a Man-sized mug brimming with beer back to the table and Pippin reacts with wide-eyed and lusty astonishment exclaiming, "They come in *pints?*" More is indeed better for Hobbits, especially when it comes to consumption of good brown ale.

For the Hobbits, however, an agreeable inn isn't just a room in which to get drunk. An inn means a cozy warm fire and a place to tell a story—a place to build friendships. It is also a meetinghouse for sharing ideas and concerns about the world. If you can't find a nice quiet pub or microbrewery in your own town, try starting a "pub night" at your house. Call forth your friends to imbibe some fine ale. Sit around a table and talk like Hobbits, face-to-face. It's a remarkably simple and satisfying way to connect.

Sustenance is so important to the Hobbits they speak in food metaphors. Before Bilbo leaves Bag End forever, he tries to explain to Gandalf the oppressive sense of hopelessness caused by his magic ring. He tells Gandalf he

✳ Who was Sauron? In the ancient days of Middle-earth the great villain of *The Lord of the Rings* was an angelic creature and a student of the god of invention. Seduced by evil, Sauron used his crafty skills to make the Rings of Power, which were intended to enslave the races of Middle-earth. After losing the One Ring, Sauron could only appear as a lidless eye ringed in fire. The disembodied Dark Lord of Mordor was incapable, therefore, of enjoying strawberries and cream.

feels like, "Too little butter spread over too much bread." Who hasn't experienced that sense of despair when you realize there's only a tiny piece of butter left in the wrapper? Not nearly enough to cover a single piece of dry toast. Dear God! Breakfast ruined! To Hobbits, an excess of butter was one of the great and requisite joys of life. The Hobbits knew what made them happy. Good friends, delicious food on the table, beer and song.

The summer after Sauron is destroyed, we are told, is one of the best growing seasons in the history of the Shire—"The Great Year of Plenty." Young Hobbits nearly "bathed in strawberries and cream." What could be better? Nothing. At least not for the men and women of the Shire for whom tasty things to eat are as good as silver and gold.✳

So what can we learn from these cheerful woolly-footed gourmands? How can we emulate them without going overboard? Hobbits could eat and drink most of us under the table, and then dance and sing while we were crawling for the door! The message here isn't about experiencing excess. Instead, it's about taking delight in what you eat and drink.

Hobbits are constantly delighted and amazed by food. They won't eat anything before first savoring it—smelling the aromas and talking about how good it's going to taste. A meal isn't a mechanical process for them. Instead it's a life-affirming event. A pleasure to share with friends and loved ones. Partner a Hobbit meal with good beer and wine and the result is usually great conversation, laughter and unbridled singing.

Treat yourself to some Hobbitish food. Find a local baker and get some huge loaves of bread and pair them with some good British cheeses (like Stilton or Double Gloucester). Go to your farmers market and stock up on garden-fresh veggies and new-laid eggs. And then pre-pare a prodigious meal a Hobbit would die for. I'll give you a hint: it must include mushrooms (see recipe for "Hobbit Stout and Mushroom Soup").* Invite your friends or family or neighbors (or all of the above!) to your home and provide them with good deep mugs of dark brown beer.

✳Recipe for "Hobbit Stout and Mushroom Soup"

Serves 4 Humans (or 2 hungry Hobbits)

2 medium-sized sweet yellow onions
5 cloves of garlic
4 Tbsp butter
3 stalks of celery (diced)
3 carrots (minced)
1 tsp fresh rosemary (or ½ tsp dried)
Salt and pepper to taste
1 lb crimini mushrooms
1 lb portabella mushrooms
3 Tbsp flour
3 cups of veggie broth
¾ cup of stout beer (I use a local microbrew from Seattle—Elysian
    Brewery's Dragonstooth Stout in a soupy salute to Bilbo's part in the
    defeat of Smaug)
1½ cups whole cream

Note: The alcohol from the stout is mostly burned off during the cooking of the soup.
But if you want it to be totally alcohol-free merely skip the addition of the beer. The
soup will be just as delicious and still fit for a Hobbit.

1. Sauté the onions and garlic in butter for a few minutes. Add the celery
and carrots along with the spices and cook until tender.
2. Add the mushrooms. Once they have started to cook down and get juicy,
blend in the flour and stir for two minutes.
3. Add the broth and the stout and simmer for 20 minutes. (Drink the rest
of the stout that's left in the bottle while you cook.)
4. Take out half of the soup, purée it in a blender, and then put this back
in the pot. (Skip this part if you don't have a blender. Your soup will be
chunkier but just as good.) Simmer for 10 minutes.
5. Add the cream to the soup. Let simmer for 15 minutes or until you just
can't wait any longer because it smells so good.
6. Serve to your fellow Hobbits with bread and cheese. Accept their praise
with modest smiles and nods of the head. Do not leave any leftovers!

Kick off your shoes. Unburden yourself with song. Tell each other tales. Dance around the table. Eat like a Brandybuck, and drink like a Took. Leave the cleaning up for the morning. Then go outside and look at the stars.

You won't regret it.

The WISDOM OF THE SHIRE TELLS US . . .

"Prosperity is not measured in gold, but rather in fine health, good company and delicious things to eat and drink."

Chapter 3

YOUR OWN PERSONAL GOLLUM

We all have someone in our lives we can't stand. Maybe it's a relative who drives us crazy, or a boss or teacher who seems to want to suck the souls right out of our bodies. It might even be a spouse or child or a pet that sends us to the edge of despair. They are masters of exasperation.

That's your own personal Gollum.＊

Gollum wasn't always called by that nasty name. At one time he was a decent sort of creature—a kind of ancestor of the Hobbits. And his name was Sméagol. He had friends, and liked to fish and tell riddles. But the power of the ring destroyed his soul, turning him into a wicked and odious wretch.

When Gandalf first tells Frodo the account of Gollum's story—

＊ Gollum was around five hundred years old when he and Bilbo had their riddle contest.

several years after Bilbo has left the Shire—the Hobbit's initial reaction is disgust. He wishes his uncle Bilbo had killed Gollum in the creature's cave in the Misty Mountains all

> * In *The Hobbit* Gollum is described as having pockets in which he kept the bones of fish and the teeth of goblins, a hunk of bat wing and "a sharp stone to sharpen his fangs on, and other nasty things."

those years ago. The wizard, however, admonishes Frodo for being so quick to pass a judgment of life or death. Gandalf thinks Gollum still has a part to play in the story. And he pities the pathetic creature and how he's been corrupted and tormented by the Ring.*

Sam and Frodo have very different reactions to meeting Gollum for the first time. Sam thinks Gollum is unredeemable and nearly everything the creature does sets his teeth on edge. As a defense mechanism he calls Gollum names like "stinker" and "sneaker." But Frodo, like Gandalf, takes pity on Gollum, recognizing how the power of the One Ring has infected Gollum's mind. He orders Sam to treat Gollum with kindness. This odd trio is forced to survive together on the long march to Mount Doom where, ultimately, Gollum betrays the Hobbits.

One of my own personal Gollums was a dog. His name was Zonker, a canine Sméagol if ever there was one. I was twenty-six years old when I rescued him from an abusive owner. Zonker was a dog who came with a lot of baggage. He snapped and snarled at children and attacked the neighbors' cats (whose poop I would catch him gnashing on like it was chewing gum). He tore apart my favorite books and barked insanely at the slightest outside noise at night, waking us from a dead sleep with the power of an electric shock. Like Gollum he skulked and cringed when he was reprimanded, and made you feel instantly guilty for your wicked cruel words. When you put a leash and collar on him he choked and gagged (just like Sméagol with Sam's Elven rope wrapped round his neck), and I could almost hear my own poor Zonker saying, "It bites us the precioussss!"

Zonker could also be incredibly affectionate and so strangely human with his big brown eyes, and his uncanny skill at performing endearing tricks. And like Gollum he was unintentionally funny sometimes—adorably brain-dead. And so my wife and I kept him and cared for him and let him drive us crazy and rule our lives for ten long years. But we loved him and treated him like our child.

Gollum acts a lot like a dog. He runs on all fours and bites when he's angry and gobbles his meat raw. Tolkien describes Gollum as *looking* like a dog when he whines and snuffles at Frodo's feet. Frodo's relationship with Gollum starts out with mercy, and the kindly Hobbit cares for Gollum like a benevolent dog-owner taking custody of a savage (but hopefully redeemable) pet that's been treated cruelly. But then their relationship becomes a twisted codependency based on their mutual love/hate relationship

for the Ring. Gollum has a big
hole of want that can only be
filled by one thing. And when he

✳ Gollum referred to the
sun as "Yellow Face."

can't get his "precious", the longing for it drives him mad.

Sam hates Gollum because he knows the creature is treacherous. Besides that Gollum is spiteful, crass and terribly needy. He's always there, like one of those annoying people who's constantly popping up unwanted. And he drives a wedge between Sam and Frodo's friendship. Nothing will ever be good, says Sam, where "this piece of misery" is around. Gollum is the antithesis of someone from the Shire. He has no manners, or sense of humor or kindness; he is completely disconnected from the world of nature, disgusted by vegetables and growing things, cursing the very sun for its light.✳

When Faramir, the heroic brother of Boromir, meets Gollum, he sees right through to the withered heart of him. He tells Frodo to part ways with Gollum because the creature is wicked and cannot be trusted and begs the Hobbit to leave Gollum behind on their journey. The courageous Faramir would rather brave any danger alone than with such a "wretched gangrel" thing alongside. Trusting him is unwise and he warns against it.

Frodo doesn't listen, of course. His fear of the unknown makes the fear of Gollum less potent. And he keeps thinking that he might be the one to change Gollum and bring him back to the light. Gandalf had said there was a spark of goodness left in Gollum, but that makes the evil Ring-controlled side of Gollum's personality more determined to snuff it out.

Tolkien knew Hebrew and was most likely familiar with the Jewish version of the zombie myth and the creature called a "golem."* Tolkien's Gollum was like a zombie—one of the undead. He has not yet "paled" like a Ringwraith, but like them he is under the control of the menacing might of Sauron. The origin of the name Sméagol also tells us something about his character. It comes from the Old English for something that "creeps." And that's Gollum, a creeping, skulking, sneaking lump of misery. Gollum is an example of the Jungian "shadow self," a character trait the famous psychoanalyst believed was present in everyone's personality: our repressed weaknesses, instincts and the cravings of the subconscious mind. Oftentimes the flaws we hate the most in others are the ones we know are lurking in ourselves.*

Of all the bad traits

---

* The "golem" of Jewish lore was created from dust or mud and animated by inscribing a special word in Hebrew on its forehead, or by writing the word on a piece of paper and putting it in its mouth.

* The Ringwraiths (or Nazgûl) were ancient kings who had been tempted by Sauron with the gift of magical rings, binding their spirits to him even after they died. They had to do whatever the Dark Lord commanded; and he in turn was helpless without them. They were Middle-earth's ultimate codependents.

Gollum possesses, the worst of them are jealousy, lack of empathy and self-obsession. These are the hallmarks of a narcissistic personality disorder. The narcissist feels threatened and rejected all the time, and retreats inside

* When playing Gollum in *The Lord of the Rings*, actor Andy Serkis's throat became so raw from doing the character's strained voice he had to concoct a special drink called "Gollum juice" made of honey, lemon and ginger.

a shell of false humility (think of Gollum groveling and submissive), while in their own mind they feel a warped sense of entitlement ("Nasty tricksy Hobbitsses!"). This particular disorder is also characterized by the psychological concept of narcissistic rage: a constant anger directed at someone else, and another layer of hatred directed at oneself. Andy Serkis, the actor playing Gollum in Peter Jackson's version of *The Lord of the Rings*, captured this split anger perfectly in the famous Gollum/Sméagol monologues.*

So what do we do when we have to deal with someone like this in our own lives—these psychic vampires who suck the life and air out of every room they enter? Do we treat them with forbearance and mercy like Frodo does with Gollum? Do we keep giving them chances until they finally—and hopefully only metaphorically—bite off our ring finger? Or do we regard them with Faramir's distrust and avoidance? Or Sam's ridicule and severity? How do we function with another person who has a great big hole of want and is demanding we help fill it, making our lives miserable?

The tale of my crazy dog Zonker was a humorous example of my own experience with a personal Gollum. But I've had many others—the human kind—in my life. And those relationships were of a far more serious nature. Stories of relationships fraught with peril are familiar and archetypal: the teacher who seems to be out to get you; the unsympathetic boss who apparently takes delight in overlooking your fundamental needs; the family member who evidently wants to hurt your feelings time and time again.

Gollums are addicted to your negative attention. They *want* you to lash out at them and become angry. They're looking for a reaction, and so one must think of a positive action to counteract their intent. Create a red herring for your personal Gollum—throw them a stinky fish. Go on the offensive with a barrage of positive distractions. Try to get inside their head and know what they're thinking before they do. Just remember, you'll need an entire bag of stinky fish with a personal Gollum because they're ravenous.*

Frodo is good at this technique. He praises Gollum constantly by calling him "clever Sméagol" and this mollifies the creature's bloated ego and humanizes

---

* The blind fish living in Gollum's subterranean pond were his favorite food. But he also ate young goblins he caught and strangled, calling them "squeakers."

him by giving him a proper Hobbitish sort of name. Sam's method of insulting and threatening him just adds fuel to the fire of Gollum's rage.

In the end Gollum cannot be changed. Even Gandalf, the stoical and thoughtful wizard, couldn't stand to be around the tiresome creature for very long (having captured and interrogated him at one point). Gollum ultimately betrays Frodo, but it's the Hobbit's compassionate and patient treatment of Sméagol that brings about the provident and happy ending of the story, and the unintentional destruction of the One Ring. Frodo fails in the quest, but does not lose his humanity by slaying Gollum. The Hobbits learn the meaning of compassion the hard way.

If we can't change our own feelings about our relationship with our own personal Gollums, perhaps we need to allow ourselves the luxury of parting ways with them. In his book *Unfinished Tales*, Tolkien wrote that the Dark Lord Sauron, having captured Gollum, detected a profound and indomitable will in the skulking and crazed little creature. A will that even Sauron could not fully comprehend, even though the Dark Lord knew what was driving Gollum's single-mindedness was his obsession with the Ring—that great hole of want that nobody could ever fill.*

* Sauron ended up letting Gollum go free, hoping the obsessed creature would lead him to Bilbo and the One Ring. But the wily Gollum was too "tricksy" even for the Dark Lord.

✳ Aragorn—whom Gandalf calls "the greatest traveler and huntsman of this age"—was the one who finally tracked Gollum down and captured him. According to Tolkien's *Unfinished Tales*, Aragorn led Gollum nine hundred miles to the Elven-king's home in Mirkwood. The journey lasted fifty days, making Aragorn the dubious winner of the "I spent the most time with Gollum" award.

So in the end we might not have any way of controlling or altering these relationships with our own personal Gollums, but we *can* master how we react to them: with forbearance, self-control, mercy, distraction and, sometimes, by going our separate ways and finding peace of mind without their company.✳

⊕be wisOom of ⊕be sbire ⊕ells us . . .

"Pity the self-obsessed Gollum in your life, for they are miserable wretches; but do not allow them to lead you on the narrow and desolate road to ruination."

Chapter 4

SLEEP LIKE A HOBBIT

Imagine a world with no alarm clocks. That's what it's like in the Shire. People get up according to the rhythm of their life. If the Hobbit is a farmer, he or she probably goes to bed a little while after sundown, and wakes up as the sun begins to rise in the morning (or when the cock crows), getting at least ten hours of sleep. A retired burglar/bachelor like Bilbo most likely stays up late and sleeps in just like his creator J.R.R. Tolkien was wont to do (see his quote at the beginning of this book).

Anybody who has suffered serious sleep deprivation, either from overworking, or insomnia, or having a new baby (the ultimate sleep-depriver), knows that a lack of sleep—even for a short period—can cause a plethora of problems: illness, depression and mild brain damage. My wife and I experienced serious postnatal lack of sleep with

✳ Gollum, once a Hobbit-like creature, had become a nocturnal cave dweller. He hated the sun, and also the light of the moon calling it, "White Face."

✳ *Flet:* the name for an Elven platform built high in a tree. After the first night sleeping high in a tree in Lothlórien, the Elves made up sleeping places for the Hobbits on the ground with soft couches, which suited the Shire-folk greatly.

one of our kids, and we actually lost the ability to speak in coherent sentences. After a few months of a colicky baby we were babbling like crazy people, or like Gollum during one of his bizarre rants.✳

Do you get enough sleep at night? Because good sleep is, without a doubt, one of the most important parts of a healthy life. The Hobbits know what is good for them and get as much as they possibly can, wherever and whenever they can get it. Their preferred place of sleep is a soft, comfy bed, of course. But they'll lie down and curl up in the top of an Elven *flet*✳ if that's the only place to get some shut-eye for the night.

Bilbo is such a sleepyhead he almost misses going off on his adventure. The day after Thorin and the Dwarves come for dinner, Bilbo wakes up well past the break of dawn, puts on his dressing gown, and inspects Bag End only to find it's empty of guests. He leisurely makes himself a hearty breakfast (which any sane person should be in the habit of doing). It's only when Gandalf shows up and tells him he's got less than ten minutes to meet up with the Dwarves at The Green Dragon that he dashes off like mad, leaving his *second* breakfast half-eaten on the table.

He doesn't get another good night's sleep for many months. In between that time he's forced to nap in a dank goblin cave with his head churning with "nasty dreams"; in the dark forest of Mirkwood, where the instant he tries to snooze a giant spider starts wrapping up his legs with web (interrupting nice dreams of "eggs and toast and butter"); or on the cold floor of the secret tunnel in the Lonely Mountain, dozing in the utter darkness, breathing stagnant Dwarf breath.* His best night's sleep comes after getting cracked on the head during the Battle of the Five Armies, and that's not saying much.

The expression "Let sleeping dogs lie" doesn't come close to describing the potential hazard of waking up a snoozing dragon. But Bilbo is so thoroughly sleep deprived after his arduous trek to the Lonely Mountain he lets a bunch of crusty Dwarves guilt him into sneaking into Smaug's hoard, where the cruel-hearted dragon is in no mood to be woken up by a funny little invisible creature smelling of Dwarf and pony— a thief who pesters him with riddles and then has the gall to steal one of his prized golden drinking cups!*

* The Dwarves and Bilbo were in the tunnel for two days.

* "Never laugh at live dragons!" became one of Bilbo's mottos. And this is a good motto for us all.

We all have the potential to make huge life-altering mistakes when we're sleepy. Like one of those people you hear about who forgets their baby at a pizza parlor, or the nuclear reactor operator who's snoozing while the big important warning light is flashing red at three in the morning. Look around at your coworkers at about four o'clock in the afternoon. Are they rubbing their eyes like little kids? Stifling yawns? Nodding off to sleep in the big meeting? Instead of going to bed at a reasonable hour these people were posting "I'm tired" on their Facebook pages late at night while simultaneously watching bad '80s movies on Netflix. For some reason adults just don't make these connections, or they're in denial about how much sleep they really need. If you're reading this book right now and you're tired, put it down and go to bed.

Bilbo makes up for all of his missed sleep with a life of leisure at Bag End. And later in life, after he "retires" to Rivendell, he spends most of his time in front of a big cozy fireplace, writing poetry and dozing to his heart's content. The Elves who are his new companions, being immortal, sleep in a different way than the Hobbit. They lose themselves in an Elven dreamworld while they "walk open-eyed in the light of this world."

We humans and Hobbits don't have the luxury of dozing while we're driving to work like the Elves would be able to do. We have hectic lives where most of us are run-

ning around like crazy in
traffic, or taking care of our
exuberant kids, or going to
school (or a combination of
all three of these). Most of
us are functioning on a serious sleep deficit, in denial

✳ The New Zealand weta (a
kind of cricket) freezes every
night in a state of chilled
slumber, only to awake the next
morning with the sun. Weta is
also the name of Peter Jackson's
special effects company
(wetafx.co.nz)

about how important sleeping really is in our lives. The
truth is it's about as necessary as eating and breathing.
Every animal in our world has to sleep—even insects and
fish.✳

One of the best ways to prepare for a delicious night of
sleeping is a hot bath. There's nothing more wonderful
than enjoying a good soaking after a day of hiking or ski-
ing or kayaking or whatever and then rolling into a soft
bed for a solid night of pillow-drooling. Hobbits love
baths. When Frodo, Sam and Pippin arrive at Frodo's new
cottage in Crickhollow, Merry has prepared tubs of hot
water for the cross-country walkers who've trekked nearly
eighty miles in three days. (Of course Pippin breaks into a
song in praise of bathing.) That night the Hobbits fall into
the deepest slumber, filled with interesting dreams.

This is another important boon of sleep: the dreamworld. If you don't go into the proper sleep cycle, your
dreams get interrupted, or never happen at all. REM (rapid
eye movement) dreaming is your brain's way of playing and

blowing off steam. A night with no REM dreams is like putting your brain in solitary confinement. When I'm getting great sleep my dreams are spectacular and fun and I wake up refreshed. I think faster on my feet the next day and I'm more creative. If I'm not getting enough sleep, my dreams are dull and repetitive; and during my subsequent waking time my thoughts become fixated on problems rather than solutions.

Many of the characters in *The Lord of the Rings* have profound visions while they're sleeping. Boromir has a prophecy in a dream telling him to come to Rivendell where he'll find "Isildur's Bane" (the One Ring) and a "Halfling" (both of which come true). Frodo has a mysterious dream of a figure trapped on a tall tower being carried away by a great eagle. It's a vision of Gandalf's rescue from Saruman's Tower of Orthanc at Isengard.*

Now I'm not saying you're going to come up with one of the greatest songs in the history of music, like when Paul McCartney dreamed up "Yesterday." Or conjure a classic work of literature, like when Mary Shelley dreamt of the idea for *Frankenstein*. But I think people who are in touch with their dreams can discover little mysteries about themselves that carry over into their waking lives and help them be more creative and present. You're receiving messages from your subcon-

* Frodo was actually seeing a flashback, because Gandalf was rescued by Gwaihir the Windlord eight days before the Hobbit's dream.

scious that your waking self might be either repressing or just overlooking.

For example, when I was nearly done with the first draft of this book, I had a dream where Ian McKellen-as-Gandalf came to me in a dream and told me, in that scolding voice we all know so well, that I had forgotten about the Grey Pilgrim as a font of wisdom in *The Lord of the Rings* and of his importance to the Hobbits. Dream-Gandalf then outlined his chapter in great detail for me. When I woke up, I quickly typed up "The Istari Protocol" (see chapter 17).

Frodo's vision of Gandalf's escape from Saruman's tower prison occurs at Tom Bombadil's house, probably one of the best places to get a good night's sleep in all of Middle-earth. When the Hobbits arrive at Tom and his wife Goldberry's little cottage they're utterly exhausted from their adventure in the Old Forest with the Hobbit-snatching tree. After dinner they fall into Bombadil's wonderfully soft beds, put their heads on the downy pillows, and pull the wool blankies up to their chins.

Bombadil speaks to them soothingly, like they're his children, telling them not to be afraid of any noises in the night. They can talk about all the scary stuff (like Ring-wraiths) in the morning, he reassures them. The next day, bright and early, old Yellow Boots Bombadil—back from a sunrise scamper over the hillsides—wakes the Hobbits up and tells them breakfast is ready. Of course they jump up and rush to the table, refreshed and ready to stuff their faces.

Scientists have proved that lack of sleep causes depression and impaired cognitive and physical function. If people are deprived of sleep for long enough, they will actually go mad, and this is one of the reasons sleep deprivation really is a kind of torture. Even Gandalf the Grey has to sleep, and he's one of the mysterious Istari.* Although the one time the wizard tries to catch a few winks with Hobbits around, it nearly leads to disaster when Pippin steals the *palantir** from right out of his hands.

* The Istari were the agents of the Valar—the god-like beings who inhabit the Undying Lands. The Istari were sent to Middle-earth in the Third Age (the period of Middle-earth history in which *The Hobbit* and *The Lord of the Rings* take place) to oppose the regeneration of Sauron. Gandalf the Grey was one of these heavenly messengers of hope.

* *Palantir:* one of the "seeing-stones" used by the ancient Númenóreans to communicate with each other across vast distances. Sort of like the "video chat" of Middle-earth.

Studies have also shown your body doesn't heal quickly when you aren't getting enough sleep. In the Houses of Healing, Aragorn uses the power of sleep to heal Faramir, Éowyn and Merry who have all been wounded by Ringwraiths and are now trapped in dark and fevered nightmares. Aragorn enters their dreamworlds and calls each of them back from the torments in which they're trapped. He's like a sleep

THE WISDOM OF THE SHIRE

hypnotherapist curing his patients of night terrors and bringing them peace of mind so they can rest and become restored to health.*

* Aragorn used an herb called "kingsfoil" to induce this mystical dreamworld connection and cure Éowyn, Faramir and Merry from the Black Breath of the Ringwraiths.

Sleep is a way to forget grief, as Aragorn says to the Companions in Lothlórien when he's "weary in body and in heart" after the loss of Gandalf in Moria. He practically throws himself onto an Elven couch and falls instantly into a deep slumber.

Frodo and Sam are so sleep deprived on their journey through Mordor it starts to break down their bodies and minds. Whenever they can they try to nap, but that's a hard thing to do, especially in the wastes of Gorgoroth where sometimes the crevice of rock is all they can find for a resting place. Sam usually ends up dreaming that he's gardening at Bag End (his happy place). Frodo's consciousness, however, is eventually taken over by the tormenting image of Sauron's flaming eyeball—a horrible wheel of fire that remains in his mind's eye when he's awake or asleep. In the end Frodo is turned into a Ring of Doom insomniac who's slowly going insane, losing touch with all of his senses. He can't remember anything about the Shire. Everything is growing dark.

After Sam and Frodo black out on Mount Doom, they're rescued by the eagles and taken to Aragorn.

* The Dúnedain were the descendants of the ancient mortals called the Númenórians. The name means "Man of the West."

The Dúnedan* uses his healing hands to put them into a kind of induced coma, sending them into a "sweet forgetfulness of sleep" that lasts almost two weeks. This is the perfect reward for their agonizing quest and feat of prolonged sleeplessness. When Sam awakens and listens to Gandalf's laughter he realizes he hasn't heard "the pure sound of merriment" for the longest time, and bursts into joyful tears. Sam is back to his old self again.

The real question for us is: how do we get more sleep in this busy world? The answer is quite simple. We need to reduce the number of distractions at night that chip away at our opportunities to get to bed at a decent hour. We have to stop looking at the Internet. Stop watching our TVs with their three hundred worthless channels. Stop torturing ourselves with worries. Just pretend kindly old Tom Bombadil is there in our room telling us, "We'll talk about all the scary stuff in the morning." And then get into bed and sleep like a Hobbit.

the wisdom of the shire tells us . . .

"Good sleep makes you healthy, happy and less likely to provoke the wrath of a dragon."

Chapter 5

DEALING WITH
"THE BIG PEOPLE"

In Middle-earth "the Big People" are the various races of Men who live outside of the Shire and are very different breeds from the Hobbits. They tower over the Halflings, as adults loom over children. To the Shire-folk, the Big People often appear sinister or oafish or merely baffling.

On occasion the Hobbits must venture into the lands of the Big People and deal with them on their terms—like in the Mannish town of Bree to the east of the Shire. In the events that take place during the War of the Ring, however, the Hobbits are totally swept up in the concerns of Men, and must leave the protection of their beloved Shire far behind.*

---

* "Strange as news from Bree" was an old saying in the Eastfarthing. Strangers who passed near the Shire were called "Bounders." The Hobbits didn't know it but the mysterious Rangers had been protecting the Shire for years.

From encounters with the sinister Bill Ferny of Bree to the enigmatic Tom Bombadil, from the grim Bard of Laketown to the imperious and patronizing Denethor of Minas Tirith, the Hobbits grow and change as they interact with the Big People. Despite their trials, the Halflings never abandon their simple goodness, sense of humor and strong moral code.

Though Gandalf is a wizard, he looks like a Man, so in Bilbo's mind Gandalf *is* a Man. Bilbo initially treats this strange fellow, loitering about his door one sunny morning, with suspicion. (Men, Hobbits believe, are slow-witted and noisy, bumbling about with the grace of goblins.) Not much good can come from dealing with Men, and that's why the Shire-folk generally keep to themselves.

Bilbo quickly learns that Gandalf is trustworthy but terribly mysterious. Hobbits are ingenuous creatures—you can pretty much read everything they're thinking on their friendly faces. They don't have the capacity for dissemblance. Gandalf is one of those people who have many secrets and hidden agendas, and if you want to be their friend you've got to just hang on tight, because you're in for a strange (but usually interesting) ride.

Gandalf, for his part, is impressed by the ways Bilbo constantly surprises him with his selfless acts of courage. After Bilbo gives up the Arkenstone* to appease

---

✳ Arkenstone: also called "The-Heart-of-the-Mountain," the white gemstone found by the Dwarves in the center of the Lonely Mountain and part of Smaug's hoard. It shined like "snow under the stars, like rain upon the moon."

the humorless Bard and the rapacious Elven-king of Mirk-wood, Gandalf is waiting in the shadows and surprises Bilbo by telling him what an excellent job he's done. The wizard, just like Bilbo, does not wish to see Thorin and the other Dwarves wiped out in a siege of the Lonely Mountain by an army of indignant Men and irate Elves. Sometimes compromise is the best way to solve an impasse with one of the Big People.

The Elves are not Men, but they offer the same sort of uncertainties for the Hobbits. When Frodo, Sam and Pippin are leaving the Shire at the start of *The Fellowship of the Ring* they meet an Elf named Gildor on the road. The Elf is humorously sarcastic for one of his kind, calling the Hobbits "dull" and gently mocking Frodo for using the Elven-tongue. Once he finds out they're pursued by Black Riders, however, Gildor becomes serious and protects the Hobbits, watching over them for the night.

When Frodo laments that a Hobbit can no longer be safe in his own country, Gildor tells him matter-of-factly that the Hobbits can fence themselves into the Shire, but they can't forever fence the rest of the world out. Gildor is a pragmatist and a pessimist. He's one of those people who laugh wryly and tell you that you're in a heap of trouble when you already know far too well. But Gildor's advice is sound. A lot of us are guilty of trying to isolate ourselves in a little protected world, ignoring what's go-

＊ Tom Bombadil was based on the character of Väinämöinen from the Finnish national poem *The Kalevala.*

ing on around us. Eventually, the Black Riders of the world will come looking for you.

Tom Bombadil is just as mysterious as the wizard Gandalf and more detached from the events playing out in Middle-earth than Gildor the Elf. In a way, however, he is the one Man the Halflings can relate to the best, for he is like a big, good-natured and friendly Hobbit in yellow boots (albeit a Hobbit who's married to a gorgeous singing river spirit).＊

Tom is the only character in Middle-earth for whom the Ring holds no power. It's nothing more than a trinket to this "Man" who calls himself the "Eldest" of Middle-earth: he was there before the Big People *and* the Little People. The Hobbits and their concerns are unimportant to Tom. He's like a preoccupied adult listening with half an ear to some children gabbing on about the complicated rules of some whimsical game they've invented.

Frodo is ticked off when Tom takes the Ring and tosses it in the air, pretending to make it vanish. And the Ringbearer becomes embarrassed when he's caught making sure Tom hasn't switched the Ring with another. He puts the One Ring on his finger and disappears from the sight of his friends, only to find that Tom can see him as plain as day: the Ring's power of invisibility doesn't work with Bombadil.

Tom is one of those rare people who can see right through us "warts and all." Although this kind of person has the power to mortify and embarrass us, they're often the most helpful type of friend for when you need plain advice without someone putting on a front and massaging your ego. The more lofty a person's position is in the world, the less likely they are to take the counsel of a Tom Bombadil—the wise man disguised as a stoner dude wearing a LIFE IS GOOD T-shirt who says exactly what's on his mind.

Soon after this encounter with Bombadil, Frodo and his friends encounter the character of Bill Ferny, a "stupid and wicked" goon in the village of Bree. They immediately take a disliking to the nefarious Ferny, especially after he charges them an exorbitant amount of money for a sad pony he's obviously starved and abused.*

We've all met Bill Ferny before. He's the kind of guy who beats his dog, tells off-color jokes and generally makes you feel uncomfortable with his leering smirk. He's not the worst sort of Man, he's just one of the nastiest—the kind who causes trouble just for fun.

* Sam named this pony "Bill" and the horse ultimately got his revenge against his namesake Bill Ferny, literally kicking the Man out of the Shire at the end of the tale with a well-placed hoof.

As they're leaving Bree, Sam hits Bill in the nose with a perfectly aimed apple. I do not advocate the use of hard fruit for violence. But every so often the Big People need a little bit of a wake-up call to see the errors of their ways. So yeah, go ahead and throw that metaphorical apple right in that smug face, if you feel so inclined.

Sometimes the Hobbits are too concerned with first impressions, however, as is the case with their opinion of Strider. None of them trust the rugged-looked Ranger when they meet him at The Prancing Pony. He's a scruffy Man, brooding and downright sketchy. While they're on the run from the Ringwraiths they learn of Strider's worth as a fighting man and a guide. They're also enraptured by his lays—romantic tales of the First Age Strider sings at the campfire. He's one of those people who "looks foul but feels fair." Like some mopey guy you meet at a party and can't stand at first, but then someone hands him a guitar and it turns out he can play any Beatles song.

Later, in Rivendell, they learn that Strider the Ranger is really Aragorn—a valorous heir to a great throne. They see him in his cool Elven clothes, probably with his hair all nice and washed, hanging out with the stunning Arwen. He's a totally different guy from that scoundrel they met in Bree. How many times in your life have you let a first impression affect the way you treat somebody, only to find you were totally off the mark? I once snubbed a new colleague because he was wearing a velvet coat that I thought looked pretentious. I immediately disliked this guy simply because of his coat. *Who in the hell wears a velvet coat?* I thought. And then all of a sudden it hit me. *Hobbits* wear velvet coats. That guy turned out to be an amazing friend, and I'm still looking for a velvet coat of my own.

In Lothlórien Frodo offers (perhaps unwisely) to give the Ring to Galadriel of his own free will, mainly because he is so enraptured with the splendid Elven queen and suddenly sees her as a means of freeing himself from the grave burden. Frodo learns a valuable lesson about seduction and the corruption of power—even the majestic Elves aren't immune to the allure of the Ring; and thus a mere Man like Boromir will become victim of an impossible-to-deny temptation.

Boromir is a jumble of contradictions. Strong of body yet weak-minded. Terrified of Sauron and at the same time as brave as a lion when in combat with the Dark Lord's servants. He fights valiantly to save the Nine Companions in the Mines of Moria, but then goes crazy and tries to seize the Ring from Frodo. Dealing with a Man like Boromir is perilous, for sure. How do you compromise with a person who wants something from you that you're not willing to give? We all can't put on a magic ring like Frodo and simply disappear.

When Frodo argues with Boromir about what course to take with the Ring, the honest Hobbit tells the Gondorian that he does not trust in the "strength and truth of Men." This is the lesson. There are strong men in the world. Powerful men who think they can wield destructive power in a way that can fix any problem. But sometimes they lie. And oftentimes their use of force is really a sign of weakness, just like it is with Boromir. Denethor's son recognizes his mistake soon enough, of course, and dies defending Merry and Pippin.

Faramir, Boromir's more thoughtful yet equally valiant brother, is strong enough to pass the character test of the Ring. His father Denethor snidely refers to him as "wizard's pupil" so we know he must have spent time with Gandalf when the wizard was in Gondor doing one of his "research trips" studying the history of the Ring.*

Frodo and Sam are understandably afraid of Faramir when they're captured by his band of Gondorian Rangers in the forest of Ithilien. But they do not beg or cower, nor do they back down. Frodo uses reason to convince Faramir to let them go, and Boromir's younger brother— the thinking-Man of Middle-earth—comprehends the perilous nature of the Ring just as well as Gandalf or Galadriel. Honesty and straight talk can sometimes work with those who have

---

* Both Faramir and his father Denethor called Gandalf "Mithrandir" which is the wizard's Elvish name.

us in their sway, especially if they are honorable and decent people.

Sometimes, however, this strategy of rationality fails.
Denethor is the perfect example of a power-hungry Man
who cannot be appeased or worked with. He's egotistical,
tyrannical and lacks empathy. A lot of us have worked for
someone like Denethor, and it's a helpless feeling to be
under the thumb of a boss like the last Steward of Gondor. Power does funny things to people's heads—and the
thought of losing that power is a heinous blow to the
bloated ego of someone used to being in complete control.

Pippin is the one Hobbit who comes into contact with
Denethor, and he instantly offers the Steward of Gondor
his life in repayment of Boromir's. The little Halfling's
forthright manner makes a crack in Denethor's armor, but
not even the goodness of the Shire can have a lasting effect
on the last Steward's impending emotional collapse. With
Men like Denethor there is no way to help them. You have
to cut your losses and run, or do what you can to prevent
them from hurting others when they finally take their fall,
otherwise you might end up in their funeral pyre.

Pippin's best friend Merry gets to interact with a Man
in a completely different way. Merry meets Théoden soon
after Gandalf helps resurrect the King of Rohan's faith
in himself and his people. The King of the Golden Hall
is the kind of person we should all be so lucky to follow:
lionhearted, kind and principled—a rare combination in

a Man. Merry offers his services to Théoden and is rewarded with a true friendship. Although Théoden is killed on the field of battle, he dies in the most honorable way for a Rider of Rohan.* His last words to Merry are beautifully gentle for one so fierce at war. He tells Merry he regrets they won't ever be able to talk anymore about "herb-lore," and asks him to think of him when he smokes his pipe.

Théoden is an archetype of heroism. He is not a perfect man, of course. He falls prey to the same fear and despair that destroyed Denethor. But when he is given a second chance at life—a pathway to redemption—he seizes it with vigor. Merry learns from Théoden to face an enemy and death without flinching.

One of the great twists in Tolkien's story is that of all the warriors of the Big People, the most valiant and pure of heart is not a Man at all, but a Woman. Éowyn, shieldmaiden of Rohan, cannot be corrupted by the diabolical council of Saruman's spy in Rohan— the odious Wormtongue.* Nor is she afraid of battle or death. Her greatest fear is

---

* Théoden was mortally wounded when his beloved horse, Snowmane, shot dead by a Ringwraith's dart, fell and crushed him. Snowmane was interred on the spot—honored with a burial mound and a poem. (The Riders of Rohan really liked their horses).

* The name of the character "Wormtongue" most likely came from the tenth century Icelandic poet Gunnlaugr Ormstunga (whose name means "Serpent-Tongue" or "Worm-Tongue").

to be trapped like a caged animal back home in Rohan, "skulking in the hills" while the men go off to fight.

* Lynn Hill is arguably the greatest woman rock climber in history. She is the first person to ever free-climb the Nose, a legendary route on El Capitan in Yosemite, California.

So she disguises herself as a male warrior in mail and helm and rides in the host with her uncle Théoden and brother Éomer, taking the surprised Merry along for the ride, seeing in the overlooked Halfling a kindred spirit who is capable of much more, just like herself.

Éowyn is Amelia Earhart, or Jane Goodall, or Lynn Hill.* She's any woman who flies in the face of a world dominated by men—men who would keep her from pushing the limits of her physical and intellectual capabilities. She doesn't defy her beloved King out of spite. She defies him because she knows he's wrong to think less of her abilities merely because she's a woman. She's uncompromising and makes her own decisions.

In one of the most thrilling and emotional scenes in *The Lord of the Rings*, Éowyn takes on the dreaded Witch-king of Angmar, an ancient sorcerer and minion of Sauron, feared by Men for thousands of years because he's never been beaten in battle. It was prophesied that no Man ever *would* triumph over him, and he mocks Éowyn with this fact as he moves in for the deathblow, eliciting her famous laughing reply, "But no living man am I! You look upon a woman."

With a little help from Merry the Hobbit, Éowyn slays the Witch-king and sends his dark spirit flying from the realm of Middle-earth and into the Void. She does so nearly at the cost of her own life, but the unshakable Éowyn would not have had it any other way. Merry learns from her more than any of the other Big People about determination and heroism in the face of overwhelming odds. This serves him well when he helps lead his own people in driving out the Shire invaders—the worst collection of Big People in Middle-earth.

the wisdom of the shire tells us . . .

"Let your moral compass point your way through the world of the Big People, and do not compromise the core of who you are."

Chapter 6

TEARING DOWN
SHARKEY'S RULES

Frodo, Sam, Merry and Pippin truly are fighting for something invaluable during the War of the Ring—for friendship and the love of the Shire. And that is why they are so crushed when they return after their long absence to find the evil wizard Saruman has taken over their small country with a gang of Big People. Saruman has imposed a fascistic strong-arm rule with the sole intent of destroying the Shire and teaching the Hobbits a lesson—a punishment for their part in the wizard's downfall.

Hobbits live in an egalitarian society where the poorest amongst them, like the old gardener Gaffer Gamgee of Bagshot Row, have the same rights and intrinsic value as the wealthiest inhabitants of the Shire, such as the famous Bilbo Baggins of Bag End. They've figured out a rule of thumb for making many things work, and they have a collective agreement to keep doing it that way. The farmer, the miller, the gardener and the innkeeper are all a part and parcel of the Shire—a sustainable and self-sufficient "nation" of independent people, all of them living and working together, never fighting amongst themselves. A place where the most important building isn't a public hall, but a public house.*

The Hobbits don't have a government. Instead they hold meetings called "moots" where the Shire-folk gather together to decide important matters and sometimes elect a nominal leader called a "thain." There are certain basic laws called the Rules that have come down from ancient times when they were reigned over by a king, but the last one of those Men died a thousand years before, and Hobbits could care less if no king returns.

They believe in free will, but there is a robust social agreement and long-standing traditions preventing people from stepping on each other's shoeless toes. The Hobbits have a deep moral code that includes the treatment of animals.*

Tolkien based the Shire on an idealized version of an England that existed before the Norman invasion of 1066, when the local population of Anglo-Saxons

* Some of the best known inns of the Shire were: The Golden Perch, The Floating Log, The Green Dragon, and The Ivy Bush.

* Hobbits, we are told, did not hunt animals for sport.

lived under a kind of early democratic monarchy. Like Middle-earth these people dwelled in regions called "shires" with "moots" and "thains." The great majority of them were industrious farmers. England was prospering in the eleventh century and had been at peace for two generations until William the Conqueror came across the Channel, killing the Anglo-Saxon king in battle, vanquishing his army, and imposing French rule and language on the defeated natives.

As a boy, Tolkien—the cheeky lad—participated in a school debate where he argued *against* the French invasion and its aftermath, like some kind of alternate-reality historian. In his fantasy the Normans lost the war and the Anglo-Saxons kept their pleasant way of life intact. Later in life Tolkien would invent his Shire—the beating heart of Middle-earth.✳

Try to imagine the Shire as Tolkien, or rather a Hobbit, would have seen it. The place is rich with natural resources—dense woodlands interspersed with fertile soil for growing crops. There is no unemployment and food is plentiful for those willing to put in a hard day's labor. It's a safe place too—a Hobbit can walk from the East to the West-farthing under starlight

✳ Tolkien attended secondary school at King Edward's School in Birmingham, England, where the school song proclaims there are "No fops or idlers" in attendance.

without fear. (Hobbits don't murder each other, at least not in the Third Age of Middle-earth.) There is no standing army or police force, only twelve Shirriffs* to patrol the entire Shire on foot, mainly to round up wayward livestock.

* Shirriff: a sort of Hobbit policeman. Based on the Old English for "shire reeve."

The Shire-folk practice sufficiency, a concept that means, "If you have enough you don't need to take any more." Businesses consist mainly of craftspeople, and these family-run enterprises remain small generation after generation, because nobody sees any need to expand them. People concentrate on the growing of food (and the eating of it), making things with their hands and living life to its fullest. They have a whiff of the Luddite about them and are wary of any machines more complicated than a loom or a mill.

There's a profound tranquility to be found here. A rhythm to the way of life that's been going on uninterrupted for over a thousand years. The Hobbits have little concern for what's taking place outside of the Shire. They very rarely venture further than the Mannish town of Bree to the east, or the borderlands to the west. From here the Hobbits can look across the rolling hills toward the direction of the sea. If the moon is out they might catch a glimpse of Elven towers atop the Tower Hills—a reminder of the Elder Days and the mysteries of the past—shimmering in the distance.

When Frodo and his friends return to the Shire after the War of the Ring they are devastated by the destruction they find. The inns have all been shut or converted into factories, and even The Green Dragon is vacated—its windows all broken. Houses are abandoned and burned to the ground. Trees have been wantonly chopped down. Ugly smokestacks pour black grime into the sky. Hobbiton has become the Detroit of Middle-earth. For Sam, this is worse than Mordor. Frodo tells him this *is* Mordor— the malice of Sauron has crept into their home.

Saruman, having lost his fortress of Isengard and his army of Orcs, now lords over the Shire with a gang of brutes who call him by the name of "Sharkey." The wizard has been enforcing his will with a set of officious orders. These are "Sharkey's Rules." We only get a glimpse of these edicts, but from the reaction of the returning Hobbits we understand they are numerous and frivolous—the malignant efforts of an evil mind to impose a bureaucratic damnation on an autonomous and freethinking people.*

Tolkien was a self-described anarchist. He wasn't your typical revolutionary, of course. He was speaking tongue-in-cheek. What he meant was he didn't want the "whiskered men with bombs" in control of the world, inflicting a way of life that defied common sense and common decency. You can see

---

* Orcs were created eons before by the evil demigod Morgoth to serve as his army in his fight against the Elves. Sharkey is an Orkish word meaning "old man."

reflections of this repugnance of despotic leaders in his stories. The venal Master of Laketown, the archetype of the deep-seated bureaucrat, is the minor villain of *The Hobbit*. He embezzles funds meant to feed the homeless and flees from his burning city, leaving his fellow citizens to die.

Denethor, the tragic figure of *The Return of the King*, is the power-hungry Steward of Gondor—an entrenched functionary—who, seeing his realm and control slipping away, abandons his constituency in their time of extreme crisis, burning himself alive, "Like a heathen king of old." Even the Steward's pompous death was an aspirational act.[*]

Saruman the wizard is an autocrat seeking power by any means necessary (like secretly creating his own hybrid army of Orcs, or placing his agent Wormtongue in Rohan). With the Hobbits, though, his influence is more insidious. He's been spying on them for decades, having grown suspicious of Gandalf's dealings with the Halflings. When he takes over the Shire the wizard knows that the way to break generous and kind-hearted people is to turn them against each other—trick them into becoming

[*] Faramir's father Denethor burned himself alive with a *palantir*, or "seeing stone," clutched in his hands. It was said if someone tried to look into that *palantir* thereafter, all they would see were Denethor's old hands withering in the flames.

spies and sneaks and tattletales, rewarding the worst kind of behavior and punishing the honorable. In that way he seizes control of a great many Hobbits with only a handful of followers at his back and imprisons all of the dissenters in isolation cells called "the lock-holes"—the Gitmo of Hobbiton.

What is Saruman creating, one wonders, inside all those factories belching black fumes and polluting the once pristine little streams and ponds of Hobbiton? We'll never know for sure. Perhaps he's just burning up all the trees out of spite, for the sheer wicked joy of making smoke. Or maybe he's making diabolical weapons to sell to Gondor's enemies—a sort of Hobbiton arms manufacturer. Whatever the case, Saruman & Co. is like an evil conglomerate that moves into a pretty little rural town, builds a factory on the river, guts the natural resources and poisons the soil and water until there's nothing left but a derelict Superfund site.

The first thing Pippin does when he sees the lists of Sharkey's odious rules posted on the walls of a Hobbit guardhouse is to rip them all down in a fit of indignation. Then he proceeds to break rule number 4 by burning up all the firewood. The Hobbits are despondent. They've gone through pain and death to come home to this devilry—these hateful stipulations. No pipe smoking! No beer! And a band of Shirriffs bickering and spewing "Orc-talk." What has become of their cherished country?

Bill Ferny, the squinty-eyed pony abuser from Bree is the first invader they meet at the newly constructed iron gates blocking the passage of the River Brandywine. The only way to deal with a bully like Ferny, Merry swiftly decides, is with the threat of violence. And the cowardly Ferny runs away as fast as he can from the Fearless Four.

The gang of murderous thugs the Companions find ensconced in Hobbiton are more violent and hell-bent than Ferny, however. And it takes a concerted effort of Hobbits, led by Samwise, Merry and Pippin to kill, capture and drive them out (and not without loss to the Shire-folk). It's a bloody and violent little revolution, and a melancholy way for the War of the Ring to finally end.

The last invader they must deal with is the despicable Saruman.* What takes place next is a kind of Shire trial where all of Hobbiton stand as witnesses and jury with Frodo acting as the judge. The Hobbits want Saruman to be put to death for his crimes, but Frodo asks the Hobbits to spare the wizard's life and send him away from the Shire and into exile. Frodo does not wish to see more savagery—he abhors the thought of his beloved and

---

* Frodo did not participate in this fight. After the Ring was destroyed he gave his sword Sting to Sam and essentially lived out the rest of his days as a pacifist.

gentle people going down a slippery slope of brutishness where they become like the merciless Saruman who (Frodo explains to his countrymen) was once of an honorable kind and might still be capable of redemption.

Saruman, humiliated by the Ring-bearer's benevolence, tells Frodo-the-judge he's become "wise, and cruel." But the wizard, his reason clouded by a corrupting lust for power, is completely in the wrong. He's become as deluded and as unprincipled as any of the Men he was sent to Middle-earth to give counsel to. Frodo's journey through the world of the Big People has indeed taught him wisdom. But Saruman is the one who is cruel, and therefore projects that hateful attribute onto others. Hobbits, at least the ones we love, do not have the capacity for cruelty, and neither should we.*

The change in our own society is less dramatic, of course, but just as pernicious as Sharkey's Rules. Our rights and privacies have slowly been stripped away through edicts such as the Patriot Act. With a deficit over 15 trillion dollars, the banksters have perpetrated the greatest fraud in the history of the world, mortgaging our children's futures for personal gain. And

---

* The actor Christopher Lee, who played Saruman in *The Lord of the Rings* and *The Hobbit*, is the only actor in the films to have actually met J.R.R. Tolkien. Lee reads *The Lord of the Rings* every single year.

corporations continue to cut away workers' rights and benefits to meet the bottom line. When are we going to tear down Sharkey's Rules in our own lives and build bridges to new and healthier ways of doing business and dealing fairly with other nations?

In the days after the "Scouring of the Shire" Sam laments that only his great-grandchildren will see the beauty of Hobbiton as it was before the desecration by Saruman. But he rolls up his sleeves and starts to work straightaway, probably with this saying of the Gaffer in mind: "It's the job that's never started as takes the longest to finish."

The Hobbits—and all of their kindred—react to the calamitous situation with the grit and determination they've shown throughout the stories . . . in just the same way humans always seem to pull together after some terrible natural disaster. The industrious Shire-folk set to their multitude of tasks, clearing away the ugly sheds and factories, cleaning up the filth, replanting and mending.

The Hobbits have come to understand they can't keep the world fenced out anymore, but at least they now know how to deal with the rest of Middle-earth. They've become a little wiser, but they've done so without tainting the essence of what makes them Hobbits—the abiding goodness intrinsic to the people of the Shire.

Sam is eventually appointed mayor of the Shire, a political position he holds for almost fifty years, until he resigns at the ripe old age of ninety-six. We can imagine

Sam was a wonderful mayor. Without a doubt more trees were planted under his tenure than any other mayor in the history of the Shire. Fireworks were certainly lit off on every public holiday and festival. Presents given out on his birthday were doubtlessly of great practicality and thoughtfulness. And I'm pretty sure the only decree he ever submitted for ratification in his long term of office was "No *new* rules."

the wisdom of the shire tells us . . .

"Baffling rules made by flawed men sometimes need to be torn down and replaced with the standards of common sense."

Chapter 7

DWARVES, DRAGONS AND
THE SACKVILLE-BAGGINSES

Bilbo has faced crazed goblins, diabolical dragons, fiendish talking spiders and a gurgling psychopath. But of all the creatures in Middle-earth, he's most afraid of two grasping Hobbits—his creepy cousins, those Sackville-Bagginses.

There's something about his cousin Lobelia and her husband Otho that just scares the bread and butter right out of poor Bilbo. It's because they want him dead, of course. Lobelia is Bilbo's natural heir, and she lusts after Bag End and all its snug glories.

It's the Sackville-Bagginses, no doubt, who declare Bilbo "presumed dead" while he's on his adventure with the Dwarves. Bilbo comes home just in time to stop an estate sale on his lawn; but he never gets back all the silver spoons Lobelia pilfered from his kitchen.

Whenever the S.-B.'s, as Bilbo calls them, come snooping around Bag End like a pair of ghouls from the Barrow-downs,* Bilbo uses the Ring to disappear

* The Barrow-downs were the ancient graves to the east of the Old Forest and were haunted by hostile ghosts guarding the treasure and bones of the dead.

and run away. Can you blame him? Is there anything more grotesque than a relative waiting like Shelob the spider for somebody to die so they can inherit all of their junk? The S.-B.'s are devastated when Bilbo takes Frodo as his heir. And they're just as delighted when Frodo decides to sell them Bag End and move away from the Shire.

Frodo, in a small effort to get back at Lobelia for all her vindictiveness over the years, drinks up all the wine in the cellars before moving out. And then, just for spite, he leaves a bunch of dirty dishes in the sink. Frodo, you see, is the least grasping Hobbit who ever lived. He never cared about inheriting Bag End. All he wanted was to be with his beloved uncle; and the S.-B.'s are an insult to familial love.

After Frodo leaves Hobbiton on his expedition to deliver the Ring to Rivendell, Lobelia's son Lotho "Pimple" Sackville-Baggins begins exporting pipe-weed to Saruman the White in return for cold hard cash. He buys up land all over the Four Farthings, sending off more and more of the Shire's food (even during a winter shortage) to

Saruman's fortress of Isengard.* Lotho is like a corrupt corporation with zero morals. He is the Goldman Sachsville-Baggins of the Shire. Pretty soon sinister Men start showing up in Hobbiton. They're ruffians who do

* Merry and Pippin happily discovered some of these provisions in the storeroom in the ruins of Isengard. They were joyous to find a barrel of Longbottom Leaf as well.

Lotho's bidding, locking up anybody who disagrees with Pimple and making a pig's breakfast of the Shire. We know what happens when Frodo, Sam, Merry and Pippin return home after the War of the Ring: they clean house, angry Hobbit-style.

Why hasn't this sort of reckoning happened in our own world? How can companies like Goldman Sachs get away with financial murder, making themselves richer than ever while millions get poorer, laughing in their sleeves and calling their own clients "Muppets" behind their backs? It's mind-boggling how a bunch of greedy Pimples run the world, while the rest of us sit back and watch them do it.

Bilbo, like Frodo, isn't a greedy or grasping Hobbit either. He's fairly well off to begin with when Gandalf asks him to be his burglar. Bilbo doesn't covet gold or jewels— he's probably never thought about them in his life. What finally gets to Bilbo is the idea of seeing something new. Mountains! Adventure! He has a map tacked to his wall with all of his favorite walks marked in red ink. Heading off with the Dwarves would mean leaving the borders of that map behind. Bilbo eventually learns, however, about the terrible Dwarven lust for precious things, and his part in that drama nearly gets him killed.

Dwarves are not evil creatures by nature. They love to work with stone and to shape material that was never alive (as opposed to the Elves who work with wood and other growing things). The joy for the Dwarves is simply in finding a vein of *mithril** or some fantastic jewel, rather than the intrinsic value of that precious discovery. The Seven Rings Sauron made for the Dwarf Lords had no power to bend them to his will and make them do his bidding. For they were an ungovernable species, even by magic, and this infuriated the Dark Lord who did everything he could to get his Dwarven Rings back once he realized his mistake.*

Sauron's Rings *did* have the power to twist the

* *Mithril* was an extremely rare and priceless metal much coveted by the Dwarves. Thorin found a small shirt made of *mithril* rings in Smaug's hoard and gave it to Bilbo. This coat of mail had been crafted ages ago for an Elven-princeling. Bilbo did not know that his "pretty thing" was worth—at least by Gandalf's reckoning—more than the entire Shire "and everything in it."

* In *The Hobbit* Sauron is referred to as "the Necromancer" and lived in the stronghold of Dol Guldur in the forest of Mirkwood.

minds of the Dwarves who wore them, causing the owners to become more fixated on rooting out gold and gems— a kind of greed amplifier. The kingdom of Erebor (inside the Lonely Mountain) was created by Thorin's ancestor while he was under the influence of just such a Ring. Fabulous wealth was unearthed, including the Arkenstone, a hypnotically shimmering jewel like a giant diamond. Eventually the dragon Smaug was drawn to the Lonely Mountain where he killed all the Dwarves and moved into their mansion. Thorin and his father were two of the few to escape.*

When Bilbo first meets Smaug (aka "the Greatest of Calamities"), the dragon has been napping on and off for 171 years inside the Lonely Mountain—ever since he gobbled up the last tasty Dwarf and burned the nearby city of Dale to the ground. Smaug has been lounging about, like a spectacularly lazy cat, on his heaps of gold and piles of gemstones, content to dream his wicked dreams. The Men of Laketown welcome the Dwarves with open arms, excited at the prospect of rivers of gold flowing down from the Lonely Mountain to the their wooden town built upon the Long Lake.*

Bilbo is terrified of the mon-

* Thorin was only 24 years old when Smaug first attacked the Lonely Mountain, and 195 years old when he returned.

* Dragon flames were not hot enough to dissolve the One Ring, though four of the Dwarven Rings of Power were melted by dragons.

ster, and he has every right
to be. Dragons can hypno-
tize you with their eyes,
freezing you where you
stand, and burn you to a
crisp before you can say,
"Bard the Bowman!" But
the Hobbit is staggered by
the sight of all of that
gold—bewitched by the

* Tolkien's poem "The Hoard"
(from *The Adventures of Tom
Bombadil* and ostensibly written
by Bilbo) describes a storehouse
full of treasure corrupting all
who come into contact with it.
The gold, the poem tells us,
cannot sing or smile like the
long-dead Elves who hid it
there, and is therefore
worthless.

"lust of the Dwarves." He also wants to snatch something
to prove to the Dwarves he's a canny burglar and not a
cowardly grocer (as Thorin insultingly calls him).

For centuries people have been fascinated by the idea
of a monster sitting on a pile of ready money. Indeed the
mythos of a dragon protecting its hoard goes back over a
thousand years to the Old English epic *Beowulf* which
Tolkien drew upon for the character of Smaug. It's a powerful symbol of miserliness—like a fat king who lolls about
on a golden throne while his scrawny servants sleep in the
straw (or a giant computer company that's sitting on a
half-trillion dollars while its workers bed down in stark
factory-managed dormitories).*

There's just something repellent about the notion of a
dragon lazing about on a mountain of cash, isn't there?
"What use has a monster for gold and jewels, anyway?" you
may very well ask. The treasure is wasted on this reptilian

gold-grubber! For us humans, however, the riches could provide so much meaning to our lives. We *need* that gold. It could give us real power. We'd be able to buy or do whatever we want!

The problem with this reasoning is that we too often equate wealth with happiness. And extreme wealth with bliss. Winning the lottery is the modern-day equivalent of finding a hoard of gold. But if the stories about the misery of lottery winners are true, having bags of money tossed into your lap is more of a curse than a boon. (You can only buy so many hot tubs).

What would you do if you found a dragon's hoard? I'd probably run around like a chicken with my head cut off, stuffing my pockets with coins and jewels, giggling insanely. But then, as my pockets got heavier and heavier, I'd start to think, *How am I going to get all of this crap back home?*

Smaug the dragon presents Bilbo with this same conundrum, and puts the poor Hobbit back on his bare heels. He mocks Bilbo asking him if he and the Dwarves had ever discussed how they were going to transport their shares of the treasure from the desolation of the Lonely Mountain. And how will they defend it from attack? Bilbo is taken aback. He'd never thought of how he was going to get one fourteenth of a small mountain of bullion to the Shire. How could he possibly make it home on such a dangerous road with "war and murder" all the way there *and* back again? A journey that nearly killed him half a dozen

> * Funeral expenses were included in Bilbo's original contract.

times just getting to the Lonely Mountain in the first place!*

The dragon is merely expressing an age-old truth faced by anyone who's lusted after wealth. The idea of striking it rich is so alluring it can drive you on and on to do crazy things in order to achieve your goal. But once you get it, you might find the burdens of the riches are too profound to bear, or not worth the trouble it took to get them. Many people ruin their health and their relationships seeking wealth. And some willingly smash their moral compasses at the start of their journey, tossing aside ethics and empathy in a grim chase for prosperity.

The Master of Laketown is the perfect example of this kind of person. The materialistic administrator misappropriates funds meant to rebuild Laketown after that city is destroyed by Smaug, and he flees into the Wastes where he ends up starving to death, scorned and alone (and no doubt still clutching his bags of gold).

Of course Smaug the dragon gets cocky and shows Bilbo his "dragon's heel," and the rest is history for Bilbo's memoirs—*The Red Book of Westmarch*. By the time Bilbo and the Dwarves enter the Smaug-less chamber and start fondling their treasure, the Hobbit has had enough. He could care less about the heaps of gold and jewels. He isn't bewitched anymore, unlike the Dwarves who can't stop pawing through the stuff. Bilbo would trade all the riches for a simple cup of fresh clean water from one of Beorn the giant's wooden bowls. When Bilbo finds the Arkenstone he pockets it on a whim.

Thorin is overcome with pride at his sudden reversal of fortune. He's reclaimed his birthright. It's taken him nearly two hundred years, but he's succeeded. This new-found sense of power puffs him up, making him more reckless and stubborn and haughty than he already was. He's totally unwilling to compromise with the Men and Elves who want a piece of the action, even though the amount he would have to give them to satisfy *their* lust would be a pittance compared to what he already owns. Thorin has become the dragon sitting on its hoard. He'll sacrifice himself and his friends simply to spite his perceived enemies.

After Bilbo sneaks into the camp of Men and Elves and offers up the Arkenstone as a solution to the stalemate, Thorin finds out and goes mad with rage. The Arkenstone was the one thing he craved more than any object in the Lonely Mountain! He grabs Bilbo and shakes him like a rabbit and is about to throw him off a high wall—dash the poor Hobbit to his death on the rocks below—when Gandalf steps in and orders Thorin to let his burglar go.

Even Thorin, however, cannot hate the lovable Bilbo forever. After the Battle of the Five Armies— after Thorin is mortally

> * The Halls of Waiting are where all the spirits of the dead in Middle-earth went after death. Each race awaited a different fate in the afterlife.

wounded and on his deathbed—he asks Bilbo for his forgiveness. The Dwarf does not want to die and go to the Halls of Waiting without making certain he and Bilbo have made peace.*

This really is the profound lesson of *The Hobbit*. Thorin goes on a quest that has dominated his thoughts nearly his entire life—to wrest back his kingdom and wealth from a dragon. All his days have been consumed with a desire for gold and power and getting his hands on the irreplaceable jewel of the Arkenstone. But in the end he realizes his lust for Smaug's hoard was meaningless. The only thing that matters, he tells Bilbo, is their friendship, which is worth far more than any precious thing mined from the ground.

Of course Bilbo can't hold a grudge. He's a "kindly little soul" as Tolkien says, and he sits in a corner of Thorin's tent near his friend's deathbed and weeps his eyes out. Bilbo has been through a lot, after all. The Hobbit thought the hardest part of this adventure would be dealing with the dragon, but the Dwarves and Men and Elves turned out to be the difficult ones to fathom.

Bilbo ends up coming back to Bag End with more than enough gold to last the bachelor Hobbit a lifetime

* At the end of the War of the
Ring, Bilbo gave Sam the last
bag of gold from the "Smaug-
vintage" in case he wanted to
get married someday.

or two. He uses the money to enjoy himself and doesn't hoard it like Smaug. Bilbo throws great parties. His wine cellar and pantries are well stocked. He takes up writing poetry and probably spends quite a bit on his library. He wears fine clothes and keeps Bag End in tiptop shape. He adopts his orphaned nephew and makes him his heir, providing him with a happy, comfortable and well-rounded upbringing.*

Frodo, though, never really gets to enjoy himself in old age like his uncle Bilbo. The War of the Ring hurts and changes him in too many ways and, surprisingly, it has done the same to his relative Lobelia Sackville-Baggins. After Saruman is defeated and his thugs cast out of the Shire, the Hobbits discover that Lobelia has been in prison for quite some time. She's well past a hundred years old now and frail from starvation. For the first time in his life Frodo feels sorry for his cousin. When Lobelia hears that her miserable son Pimple was murdered by Wormtongue, she is heartbroken and moves out of Bag End and Hobbiton forever.

Lobelia's miseries have made her a more empathetic Hobbit, however. She has learned compassion for other Shire-folk, and is no longer avaricious. She takes all of the ill-gotten money that belonged to her son and gives it to Frodo for him to start a sort of foundation: a Shire NGO, if you will, that builds new homes for the displaced victims of Saruman's destructive invasion. It's Hobbitat for Humanity.

The twenty-first century has produced an exponential growth in materialism. Nowadays it seems like the only people who are held in high regard are the super wealthy. It's not enough to be a millionaire anymore. Billionaires are where it's at. And people will do anything, it appears, to claw their way to the top of the dragon's heap of gold. Gordon Gekko (as played by Michael Douglas) was enlisted twenty-five years after the movie *Wall Street* to recant his "Greed is good" slogan in a video campaign created by the FBI in 2012—an effort to curb rampant insider trading.*

Greed, for lack of a better word, sucks. And money really can't buy you love.

My wife and I got married twenty years ago when we were still in college. We didn't have enough money to buy new shoes, let alone pay for a wedding. So we had a barefoot ceremony in my parents' backyard. Our generous friends and family brought food and drinks and we all danced together on the grass. Who needs new shoes when you've got true love and friendship?

* In an article in *Forbes* ("How Much Is a Dragon Worth, Revisited," April, 2012), editor Michael Noer attempted to calculate the net worth of Smaug's hoard in today's dollars. He came up with the value of $62 billion (including $3.9 billion for "diamonds embedded in dragon").

The Hobbits, who hardly ever wear shoes, would understand exactly what I'm talking about.

ᴄʜᴇ ᴡɪѕᴅᴏᴍ ᴏғ ᴄʜᴇ ѕʜɪʀᴇ ᴄᴇʟʟѕ ᴜѕ . . .

"Greed is for bewitched Dwarves, avaricious dragons, and gold-loving Sackville-Bagginses."

Chapter 8

THE LORE OF THE ENTS

When Old Man Willow, the vindictive tree who lives in the Old Forest at the edge of the Shire, traps Merry and Pippin inside his gnarled trunk, we are introduced to a crucial aspect of Middle-earth: the Hobbits (and other sentient creatures who inhabit Tolkien's world) are in a unique relationship with the natural world—a relationship where the scales could tip in either direction.*

In our world we like to believe we are the masters of nature. In Middle-earth, however, the wise know better. Here, nature can fight back.

Trees held great import for Tolkien. When he was a child he enjoyed having long conversations with favorite trees. Later in

* The name "Ent" comes from the Old English for "giant." The Ents resembled enormous tree-like humans.

life, in a moment of exasperation, he wrote he would welcome *Ragnarok* (the mythological apocalyptic battle between the Norse gods) if only it would wipe out all the ugliness of our industrialized world and bring back his beloved and diminishing forests.

It is no small wonder that trees play momentous roles in Tolkien's stories, both as living characters and as symbols. Mirkwood, the Old Forest, Lothlórien and Fangorn are more than just set pieces for the action—they're epicenters of mystery and magic with rich histories hearkening back to the genesis of Middle-earth.

Tolkien's Ents are some of the oldest inhabitants of his fantasy world, and some of the strangest as well. They were created by one of the Valar (the ancient demigods of Middle-earth) to serve as protectors of the forests. Later, the Elves taught the Ents to speak (apparently because the Elves just loved to chat with trees and finally wanted them to start saying something back). The Ents wandered the woodlands of Middle-earth—like humungous and powerful forest rangers in a national park.✳

At some point the Ents lost contact with the females of their species and became isolated from the rest of Middle-earth as the great forests shrank over the millennia, remaining only in

✳ Treebeard might have talked slowly, but he walked fast. He carried Merry and Pippin "seventy thousand Ent-strides" across Fangorn Forest, or nearly one hundred miles in one day (about 7.5 feet per stride).

their stronghold of Fangorn. Here they live in a sort of egalitarian society similar to the Hobbits with Entmoots* being their primary method for communicating with one another. It's at one of these gatherings where they make the collective decision to attack Saruman's stronghold at Isengard, thus turning the tide of the War of the Ring.

Treebeard tries to impress upon Merry and Pippin (who come under his care when they escape from the band of Orcs who've captured them) the importance of not being too hasty. To the Ents there is a particular kind of insufferable foolhardiness in being impatient and impetuous. The Ents live as long as the longest-lived trees, after all, and plan for hundreds of years in the future rather than merely reacting to what is happening at this instant. In this respect the Ents are masters of sustainability.* A hundred years is nothing to them.

We humans could learn a lot from this kind of far-reaching vision. In our world it seems like corporations and politicians are far too eager to sacrifice the last remaining wilderness areas around the globe to tap cheap

* The folkmoots of Anglo-Saxon England and Europe were "meetings of the people" where the free men of a region came together to discuss matters of importance. Often these assemblies were held under the boughs of a gigantic tree.

* Sustainability is a model of development and a way of life that doesn't compromise the ability of future generations to fulfill their own needs.

carbon fuel sources to run insatiable factories. Oil and coal companies are just like the corrupted wizard Saruman who cuts down Fangorn Forest to fuel the twisted machines he's built inside the black walls of Isengard.

When Legolas enters Treebeard's forest of Fangorn for the first time his Elven nature-empathy meter goes off the charts. He feels the living presence of the trees so strongly it takes his breath away. He perceives an overwhelming force of primeval memories. The forest thinks. And he can sense an anger growing here—a mounting fury in response to the evil that's wreaking havoc outside of this woodland realm. Legolas, we learn later in the story, can actually understand what trees are thinking if he is only given enough time to commune with them. If only we could listen to our own natural world in the same way.

Lothlórien is another tree-filled wonder. When Frodo is brought to the last bastion of the Noldor✶ in Middle-earth he is overcome by the sight of the towering silver *mallorn* trees. Everything appears magnificent and radiant to his eyes, as fresh and new as if it had been suddenly created at that moment, and yet at the same instant as old as time itself. Sam describes it best when he says in awe, "It's like being inside a song."

There are places like this in our world that are filled with trees

---

✶ The Noldor were the Elven Kindreds who exiled themselves from Valinor and came to Middle-earth.

so fantastically beautiful they defy reason. Anyone who has stood beneath the towering redwoods of Stout Grove in Northern Califor-

* You can visit Stout Grove in California's Jedediah Smith Redwoods State Park located in Northern California near Crescent City.

nia, or gone "leaf-peeping" in Vermont during autumn have a sense of what the Hobbits were feeling. The sensation is something akin to a spiritual epiphany. And the sound of tree limbs creaking and swaying in the wind is indeed like being inside a song of the earth.*

In his essay "On Fairy-Stories" Tolkien wrote about the importance of fairytales in his own childhood because they gave deep and magical meaning to commonplace things he might have overlooked in everyday life, such as trees. Think of all the tropes from history associated with this simple word: the tree of life, family tree, tree of knowledge. The word "tree" for Tolkien meant more than just a big plant that sprouts from the earth. It was a living thing firmly rooted to the history and mythos of humanity (and therefore it had to play a great part in the history of his invented realm).

In the story of Middle-earth's ancient origins, as told in Tolkien's epic tale *The Silmarillion*, one of the first violent acts perpetrated by the evil demigod Melkor (the master of Sauron) is to destroy the two gigantic radiant trees that light up the world of the Undying Lands. In an

* Melkor was so hated by the Valar they changed his name to Morgoth (meaning "all darkness"). His spider was called Ungoliant and was the progenitor of Shelob.

act of jealousy and hatred he stabs the two trees with his spear, then orders his giant spider to suck out the sap and refill them with its toxic poison. The trees, needless to say, never recover. It's Melkor's equivalent of causing a nuclear meltdown.*

The Gondorians plant a descendent from a cutting of one of these beauteous trees high atop the citadel of Minas Tirith to serve as the symbol of their people. The White Tree, as it is called, flourishes for years, until at last it too withers and dies after the passing of the last King of Gondor. After Aragorn claims the throne, Gandalf takes him up to the nearby mountains where he shows him a sapling growing in the snow—a scion of this long-dead tree miraculously poking through the crust of ice. Aragorn replants the tree in place of the dead one. It's an allegory of renewal and rebirth for the New Age of Middle-earth.

At the climax of *The Two Towers* the Ents are forced to make a fairly quick decision (which goes against every fiber of their fibrous beings) to defend their beloved forest from the axes of the White Wizard's Orcs. Saruman has been cutting down their beautiful groves. They've seen the desolation near Isengard. Treebeard says that Saruman has "a mind of metal wheels." The wizard cares not for growing things, and what's worse, he's been meddling with Orcs—changing them so they no longer fear to walk in daylight. Saruman is practicing genetic engineering! Isengard is the Monsanto of Middle-earth.*

* Monsanto is a multinational agricultural biotech conglomerate that has come under attack for its genetically engineered seeds and its herbicide Roundup.

Treebeard rebukes himself for not acting sooner. He's grown complacent, he realizes, and let Saruman get away with one outrageous desecration of nature after another. The Ents storm Saruman's walls, ripping apart stone "like bread-crust" and squashing the enemy underfoot, then destroy a dam, flooding Isengard and putting out the wizard's furnace fires once and for all. The revenge of the Ents is terrifying and swift. Saruman should have known better than to kill trees protected by the great shepherds of Fangorn.

In our own lives the natural world is under assault. Our watersheds and forests (and we humans) are being poisoned by heavy metals from coal-fired power plants around the world, and global climate change is increasing due to our reliance on carbon-based energy sources. If we don't change our ways, our trees might finally get fed up and come after us like an army of enraged Ents.

There are people who put themselves on the line, however, and challenge the status quo of the Sarumans of our world. Like Julia Butterfly Hill, a fan of *The Lord of the Rings* as well as trees, who lived in the top of a 180-foot tall redwood for over two years to keep it from getting cut down. Or the former Maldives president Mohamed Nasheed, who was named a Champion of the Earth for his efforts to educate the global community about climate change, showing his vanishing island archipelago to the world—a compelling symbol of the threat of rising sea levels.

These two people have made a difference in a big way. But you can do your part without living in a tree or traveling the world as a diplomat of change. Find out what the environmental issues are in your area. Hold your city and county council members to a high standard, as well as your state legislators, governor and senators. Write an opinion piece (op-ed) for your local newspaper about issues that concern you, and call your representatives to let them know how you—one of their valued constituents—feel about what's going on in your region. Use social media sites to inform your friends about the real news that's happening in the world, not just what the media chooses to filter your way.

At the end of *The Two Towers* Frodo and Sam are just about to enter the Land of Mordor when they pass through a place called the Crossroads—the easternmost edge of the Realm of Gondor. Here stand a line of ancient trees, their tall tops blackened from repeated lightning strikes (courtesy of the evil magic of Sauron). But though the tops are dead and twisted, Frodo observes, there is still life in these august entities standing like sentinels of resistance to the evil of Mordor.

These are the last trees they will see on their journey to Mount Doom. There

* The eagles carried Frodo and Sam to Ithilien—the easternmost province of Gondor. After Aragorn became King he gave this region to Faramir and his new bride Éowyn.

are no trees growing in Mordor, only brambles and thickets—the same invasive plants that take over lands in our own world after a clear-cut. After the Ring is destroyed, Sam and Frodo fall into unconsciousness on the ruined slopes of Mount Doom. They're rescued by the eagles and carried far away from the desolate lands.* The very first thing Sam sees when he opens his eyes are the beautiful swaying boughs and branches of beech trees in daylight. He feels wonderful, he says, like "the sun on the leaves!"

He's back in the land of the living. He's back amongst the world of trees.

the wisdom of the shire tells us . . .

"Heed the advice of Ents and never be too hasty, but like them act swiftly in defense of what you believe is right."

Chapter 9

THE COURAGE OF A HALFLING

In the prologue to *The Lord of the Rings* Tolkien informs us that the Hobbits are not a warlike people. The Shire-folk have gone to battle only a few times in their entire history (and that was long ago); and they've never waged war against each other. All of the weapons they used in the olden times are rusted and hanging over fireplace mantels, or collecting dust in the Shire museum.*

How did the Shire produce so many doughty warriors— some of the greatest heroes of the War of the Ring—with such a peace-loving atmosphere? Maybe it's because the Hobbits were fighting for something quite different than glory or bloodlust— they were fighting for the love of their friends.

* The Shire museum or "Mathom-house" was in the town of Michel Delving near Hobbiton. Bilbo let them display his *mithril* coat for several years.

"There is a seed of courage," Tolkien wrote, "hidden (often deeply, it is true) in the heart of the fattest and most timid Hobbit, waiting for some final and desperate danger to make it grow."

I think everyone has this "seed" inside of them, just waiting for the right circumstances for it to come to life. The reason we relate to Bilbo is because, like most of us, he reacts to the terrifying events of his adventure the same way we would: with out-and-out fear! At the start of *The Hobbit* Bilbo is not what one would call "brave." In fact, he's a quivering jelly of a coward, even by Hobbit standards, shrieking in fear at inopportune moments (much to the disgust of the dauntless and battle-hardened Dwarves).✱

Like a lot of older confirmed bachelors, Bilbo has become entrenched in routines that revolve around pleasing himself: eating, drinking, smoking his pipe, etc. He's remarkably shiftless (at least by a busy wizard's standards), obsessed with his well-stocked pantry and starting punctually each of his many meals during the day. His chief concerns are keeping the hair on his wooly feet tidily brushed and the brass doorknob on Bag End's front portal shining brightly in the sun.

We all know somebody like this in our own lives. The committed single

---

✱ Thorin Oakenshield fought in the War of the Dwarves and Orcs where he became famous for using an oak branch to defend himself after his shield was shattered, thus earning his surname.

---

* After his adventures with the Dwarves, Bilbo invited them to come and visit anytime, even though, he reminded them, tea was at four o'clock.

person obsessed with the minutiae of their own daily routine. They have become their own inner child, and they're as inflexible and worried about someone invading their space as is Bilbo when Thorin's gang of Dwarves descends upon his snug little Hobbit-hole, plunging his world into chaos (not to mention cleaning out his pantries without so much as a "Please" or a "Thank you").*

So why does Gandalf choose Bilbo to join in his adventure with the Dwarves? Was it mere chance that he walked by Bag End on that sunny day and used a spike on the bottom of his staff to scratch Bilbo's round door with the rune "G" for Gandalf? Perhaps the wizard had had a premonition that he needed to check up on Bilbo Baggins whom, we must assume, he'd watched off and on for the Hobbit's entire life. There was just something about Hobbits that Gandalf liked. Perhaps he sensed that "seed of courage."

For the first part of the journey to the Lonely Mountain Bilbo is a terrible companion. He's constantly whining about the depredations they're facing. "My stomach feels like an empty sack," he whines to Thorin. And not only that! By the Bullroarer's wooden club he's missing picnic season and blackberry picking back home! (Bilbo "Berries" Baggins wasn't exactly the toughest burglar to send into the den of a murderous dragon—bless his furry feet).✳

The first time Bilbo shows real heart is when Thorin & Co. get captured by the giant spiders in the forest of Mirkwood. Bilbo

✳ Bilbo was a proud descendent of the famous Bullroarer Took who invented the game of golf when he struck off an invading Orc's head with a wooden club, sending it rolling into a hole.

✳ Sting was made by Elven-smiths from Gondolin thousands of years before Bilbo found it in the trolls' cave.

reacts without thinking, slaying his first monster—a dark-blooded arachnid—and instantly swells with pride, giving his little Elven sword the winsomely Hobbitish name "Sting."✳ After that he takes on an entire army of the vicious talking spiders single-handed, slaying dozens of them while cutting free his companions, then defends the poison-addled Dwarves while they retreat to safety. This is real hero's work!

Sneaking into Smaug's lair was also brave—that goes without saying (though Bilbo was sort of shamed into going there in the first place by those wily Dwarves). Bilbo's next moment of real courage, however, is when he takes the Arkenstone jewel, sneaks over the wall of the Dwarves' makeshift fortress, and delivers it to the King of the Woodland Elves. Bilbo knew his act would gall Thorin, possibly stirring up a murderous wrath in the Dwarf who was obsessed with finding the jewel. But Bilbo wanted to stop a pointless war from happening—from seeing his friends cut down for no good reason.

Whistleblowers and other people who fight corruption exhibit this kind of altruistic courage, putting their own careers (and sometimes their lives) on the line when they expose government waste, fraud or widespread abuse in a system. It takes a brave person to risk antagonizing someone in a position of power, knowing they will bring down the hammer of wrath upon their own head.

Frodo also possesses a fearlessness that he didn't know he had. Both Bilbo and Gandalf knew it was inside him, though. They considered him to be "the best Hobbit in the Shire." After Frodo and his friends leave Tom Bombadil's they get lost in a magical fog and end up trapped inside an ancient tomb—in the mound of a Barrow-wight.*

The evil creature haunting the barrow puts Merry, Pippin and Sam to sleep and arrays them for a sacrificial killing. Despite the crazed fear in his heart, Frodo feels the courage rise inside him. He refuses to run away and abandon his friends (though he imagines, for an instant, doing just that). He picks up a nearby sword and hacks off the wight's giant hand as it's reaching round the corner of the tomb.

Sam has a similar moment when he attacks the monstrous spider Shelob,

---

* The Barrow-wights could reanimate the corpses of the dead.

stopping it from carrying the cocooned body of Frodo away and feasting upon his corpse. The "seed of courage" that Tolkien wrote about was inside this simple gardener too. Just as it springs to life in Merry when he attacks the Witch-king of Angmar on the battlefield in front of Minas Tirith, stabbing him in the back of the leg (the most successful back-of-the-leg assault in literature since Achilles' pierced heel), stopping the Lord of the Nazgûl in his undead tracks, allowing Éowyn to move in and slay it, banishing its evil spirit forever.✳

Shelob and the Witch-king were not prepared for something so small to attack, and they certainly didn't expect the little Hobbits to fight with such ferocity. We all have the capacity to surprise the bullies of the world and take a stand. And there are many ways to fight other than using your fists (or Elven swords forged in Gondolin). Simply voting in an election is a strong way to send a message in a democratic society. All those votes add up, and sometimes the outcome surprises the hell out of the people in charge. Taking to the streets and demanding change also seems to be a viable option, as demonstrated by courageous protestors around the world asking for change to their repressive governments.

✳ The Witch-king was an ancient sorcerer who willingly took one of Sauron's "Nine Rings for mortal men doomed to die." It was prophesied that no man would kill him. Instead it took a shield-maiden and a Halfling.

The Hobbits not only have courage themselves, they inspire it in others. Boromir dies trying to save Merry and Pippin from the Orcs, slaying a heap of the enemy fighters until his sword is broken and he is pierced with arrows— enough shafts to fell several warriors. Even though he gives up his life in a failed effort, he redeems himself for trying to take the Ring from Frodo, and the spell that had seized him vanishes, letting him die in peace in Aragorn's arms. Aragorn, for his part, refuses to give Merry and Pippin up to be tormented by the Orcs, and sets out with Gimli and Legolas on an ultra-marathon across the plains of Rohan, knowing they are chasing an overwhelming force into unknown territory, but completely unfazed by the danger.*

Part of being brave is the ability not to panic under extreme duress like Aragorn, Gandalf and the Hobbits demonstrate time and again. I put myself squarely in the "chicken" category, but the few times I've faced real danger something has clicked in my brain, calming me down enough so I could think myself out of trouble.

I was on a SCUBA adventure once, following my buddy through a narrow and twisting lava tube in which I'd never been before, when my only light suddenly went dead. The flashlight just faded to nothing. The last thing I saw was a glimpse of my friend's fins kicking as he

---

* Aragorn, Legolas, and Gimli ran for four days straight averaging thirty-three miles per day.

went on ahead into the utter blackness, oblivious to my plight. I tried to move forward but somehow I'd become stuck in place, like a cork in a bottle.

There I was, alone in the most unfathomable darkness I'd ever known, fifty feet under the sea with the back of my oxygen tank caught on a low-hanging rock, immobilized and with only a few minutes of air left to breathe. There wasn't enough room to move my arms, let alone turn around. The only thought in my mind was of my wife and how I wanted to see her again.

I flashed on an argument we'd had before I'd gone on this trip when I'd told her I didn't want to have children at this time in our lives because it would take away my precious freedom. She'd cried and told me she couldn't believe I was so selfish. Now, I wondered what had I been thinking. What an idiot I'd been. Of course I wanted to have kids with her! I didn't want to die alone in some dark hole under the sea. Was this how my story would end? If so, this was a pitiful way to go.

Strangely enough I didn't freak out. That would have used up all my air and killed me. Instead I breathed calmly, wriggled myself free (after a few of the longest minutes of my life) and crawled blindly forward through the lava tube until, at last, I saw a glorious blue glow appear in the distance—the tube's exit. I would live to see *real* courage: my Amazon warrior of a wife giving birth to our two kids.

I'd put myself in that dangerous diving situation for the thrill of adventure. But there's a special kind of valor when someone knows they are going to die carrying out an order. Frodo journeys into Mordor believing he won't ever be going back to the Shire. He's like a soldier heading off to the front lines in a killing zone. Sam is just as brave. About fifty miles from Mount Doom he realizes they are never going to make it back to the Shire. As his hope for survival dies, his resolve hardens like never before. He feels as if he were "turning into some creature of stone and steel" that nothing in Mordor could thwart. There are many chances to turn back, but none are taken. The only option is to move forward toward the goal.

At one point in their ascent up the towering stairs of Cirith Ungol, Frodo and Sam pause to rest. Sam, in his typically optimistic mood, wonders aloud about what kind of tale they've landed themselves in. How will their story turn out? Will anybody know or care what happened to them? The best tales to be in, Sam muses, are the ones with happy endings, but sometimes they're not the most interesting to hear told. It's one of the best scenes, in my opinion, in all of *The Lord of the Rings*—a mirroring of the story within a story.

Frodo tells Sam that one of the main characters of this great tale would certainly be "Samwise the stouthearted." And stouthearted he is, forging on to the end of the story, where catastrophe suddenly and happily turns to *eucatastrophe**—the shattering of the tower of Barad-dûr and the downfall of Sauron.

> * *Eucatastrophe*: Tolkien's invented term from two Greek words meaning a "good calamity."

When someone is going through a difficult or terrifying time in their life, whether it's fighting for survival in the world of business, or perhaps fighting for survival on real battlefields, the human response is to wonder if anybody cares or understands what they're suffering. True bravery is forging ahead, like Sam and Frodo, understanding that no one might ever know your tale and what you're going through. Facing a difficult trial and growing as a person is the true reward.

the wisdom of the shire tells us . . .

"There's a seed of courage in all of us, waiting for the right time and place to spring to life."

Chapter 10

THE GAFFER'S GARDEN

There's a deep interest amongst the Halflings concerning horticulture, and not just the propagation of *Old Toby's Leaf*. Therefore, as one might expect, one of the most respected jobs in the Shire is that of the gardener.✶

Bilbo's chief gardener is the old Gaffer Gamgee✶ whom Bilbo refers to with the honorific "Master," and with whom he is constantly consulting upon the important questions of growing vegetables—especially

✶ Meriadoc Brandybuck was credited as the author of *Herblore of the Shire*. The best varieties of pipe-weed were thought to be: Longbottom Leaf, Old Toby, and Southern Star.

✶ The Gaffer Gamgee was most likely based on the real-life position of the Victorian-era chief gardener of a country estate who held the same lofty status as the head butler. The Gaffer tended Bilbo's garden for forty years.

potatoes. Hobbits love boiled tubers like dragons crave roasted Dwarf.

Bilbo would have got much of the food he ate from his own land, and the Gaffer would have done all of this important work along with his son and apprentice Sam at his side. Bilbo leaves the Shire after his one hundred and eleventh birthday to go live in Rivendell. But before he departs, he bestows several gifts upon the Gaffer: two sacks of potatoes, a new spade and some ointment for rheumatism—no doubt caused by decades of digging Bilbo's soil!

After Frodo sells Bag End and departs the Shire with the Ring, Sam comes along with him under the pretense he'll be tending his master's new garden at Crickhollow Cottage in Buckland. When they get to Lothlórien, however, the clairvoyant Elven queen Galadriel doesn't need to be told Sam is a gardener. She immediately recognizes Sam's gift as a grower.*

The Shire and its folk, as I pointed out earlier, are idealized versions of early Medieval England and its farmers. During that time period most people lived in

* Sam received a special gift from the Elven Queen before departing from Lothlórien: a small box with a silver Elvish rune on the lid. The rune was in the shape of a "G" for "Galadriel" but, she told him, it could also stand for "garden" in the language of the Shire. Inside were a few pinches of soil infused with her powerful magic, and the seed of a *mallorn*—the magnificent trees of Lothlórien.

* This type of construction is called "wattle and daub." little houses made of a mixture of soil, sand, clay and dung spread over a lattice of woven branches.*

These earthy homes, like aboveground Hobbit-holes, were surrounded on all sides by a small garden space—a cottage garden. This is where the farmers could grow food exclusively for themselves, as opposed to the crops they grew in common fields with their neighbors.

Tolkien referred to Sam—his favorite character—as "the jewel" of Hobbits. It might be argued he is the real hero of *The Lord of the Rings*. Tolkien's works are filled with other doughty agriculturalists, like the eponymous hero of his story *Farmer Giles of Ham*, a good-natured plump farmer (just like Sam Gamgee) who is drawn into a great adventure. In *The Lord of the Rings* two other agronomists—Farmer Cotton and Farmer Maggot—both make brief but important appearances.

In *The Fellowship of the Ring* the Gaffer actually has a conversation with one of the Black Riders, and the plucky old Hobbit faces up to the terrifying creature without running and cowering inside his hole like any sane Big Person would have done. The Gaffer would probably have been more afraid of potato blight than the undead Nazgûl's Black Breath.

Let's take an imaginary tour of what a Hobbit-hole garden might have looked like in its prime. By the Shire reckoning it's the month of *Wedmath* (mid-August).* Imagine you're standing in front of a little handmade

* *Wedmath* is derived from an Old English name meaning "month of weeds."

wooden gate that opens into a patch of sunny yard that's surrounded by a low fence made of woven branches. You open the gate and walk under an arbor thick with hanging clusters of grapes—you can reach up and pluck some as you pass. The grapes are the fattest and juiciest you've ever seen, for this is "The Great Year of Plenty"—the summer after the downfall of Sauron.

You enter the garden and are bathed in sunlight. Every inch of the little yard is filled with raised beds and pots bursting with growing things: mounds of earth topped with thick potato leaves and dotted with white blooms, tripods constructed from apple suckers supporting bean and pea tendrils snaking toward the sky, the tops of purple-red beets poking from the soil and tall sunflowers with their faces turned toward the path of the sun.

At the far end of the northern side of the garden is a brick wall. Fruit trees have been trained to grow against the wall to catch the heat radiating from the bricks. These trees have taken the gardener years to prune and train into their intricate shapes. Their production of fruit is extended significantly because the trees are able to absorb the maximum amount of solar energy.

Everywhere is the loud drone of honeybees at their work. Bees are an integral part of a cottage garden. These insects provide the gardener with honey (Tolkien was quite fond of honey in his tea), as well as playing one of the most important roles in agriculture—they pollinate all of the plants. The gardener keeps his bees in several big overturned woven straw baskets.* And everywhere—in pots, along the edges of vegetable beds, even stuffed into the cracks of the brick wall—flowers and herbs are in full bloom. These supply the bees with pollen and nectar when the vegetables aren't in blossom.

* In Anglo-Saxon England these bee-baskets were called *skeps*.

The gardener spends most of his day here, hoeing the weeds and watering. In the afternoon he lets his chickens out of their coops and they wander about eating harmful insects from off the vegetables and providing a constant source of fertilizer. A curious crow alights on the fence and nods his head, cawing in a friendly way, while a robin red-breast and his mate dig in the soil for grubs, always keeping one eye on the lazy cat curled up in a patch of sun, swishing her tail contentedly.

Later in the day the gardener sits with his back against the warm brick wall, eating a slice of the missus's warm bread, enjoying a pint and puffing on some pipe-weed. He smiles as he blows the bluish vapor toward the sky, thinking of Gandalf's famous multicolored smoke ring tricks.

It sounds like an enchanting place, doesn't it?

The first time I helped make a garden I was in my twenties. My wife and I were newly married and renting a tiny old house directly behind a parking lot. In our backyard was a derelict patch of grass about the size of a small bedroom. We got permission from our landlord (a diminutive Hobbity sort of woman we called "Mrs. Sniff" because of her habit of sniffing all the time) to turn this unused space into a garden.

Everything we planted in that little place grew like it had been dusted with Galadriel's magic soil. We had enormous Brandywine tomatoes (planted in honor of the Brandywine River, of course) and cucumbers fat and sweet. There were delicious lettuces and enough basil to make dozens of pesto dinners. It had all been so easy. We simply stripped off the sod, turned the soil, mixed in some compost we got from the local feed and seed, planted some seeds and watered. We had no idea what we were doing. But we were on our way to creating our first cottage garden—like a little piece of the Shire.*

* Uprising Seeds (uprisingorganics.com) and Territorial Seed Company (territorialseed.com) are two small but industrious seed companies selling non-genetically modified heirloom seeds such as Brandywine tomatoes and rainbow chard.

During World War II Britons, Canadians and Americans were encouraged to grow victory gardens to supplement their meals because of the intense rationing. President Roosevelt

* The first year after First Lady Michelle Obama created the White House garden (in 2008) the planting of home gardens went up nearly twenty percent in the United States.

put one in on the White House grounds. People dug up their yards and planted vegetables. In the United States during those war years, nearly 50 percent of the country's produce was grown in these small gardens.*

Tolkien spent a lot of time in his garden during WWII, and kept chickens, scrounging difficult-to-find wood and recycled nails to build his coops. There's an urban chicken movement going on right now. Thousands of people are keeping chickens (and sometimes ducks) in cities, while other city and suburban dwellers are discovering how to raise bees for the production of honey and beeswax.

After the collapse of the Soviet Union in the early '90s Cuba lost its steady supply of diesel fuel to run its big farms. The population of Havana—where two-thirds of Cubans live—faced with drastic food shortages, had to turn quickly to the idea of urban farming. Three hundred thousand patios, backyards and lots were rapidly turned into gardens. A little over twenty years later, Cuba is using half the diesel fuel to feed the same number of people, and they're doing it without pesticides or petroleum-based fertilizers. Oxen were reintroduced to do field work, providing free manure.

The Hobbits, we must remember, would have done all

of their labor by hand or with the aid of hoofed animals. The most complex machines at their disposal, Tolkien tells us at the beginning of *The Hobbit*, were water mills and forge bellows.

Try digging yourself a small garden bed and see how satisfying it feels to look at the newly turned earth just waiting to be planted. You'll know why Sam keeps dreaming of his garden while in the barren wastelands of Mordor. (Instructions on how to make your own Hobbit garden can be found at the end of this book.)

After the Shire is liberated from Saruman, Sam sets out to make repairs. To him that means getting things growing. "Where there's life there's hope," as the Gaffer always used to tell him. Sam, clever Hobbit that he is, uses Galadriel's gift of magic soil one grain at a time, spreading the potent dust all over the Shire.

He plants the *mallorn* tree seed by the stump of the Party Tree and patiently waits for spring. The sapling that springs up from the ground is so healthy and fast growing it nearly leaps from the dirt—a sturdy silver-barked wand. There will be another Party Tree. A place to celebrate life. For the Shire-folk—who are so totally connected to the land where they live—nothing could be as momentous as this resurrection of the natural world.

Happily, we don't need magical dust to make things grow. But maybe it's a good idea to go back in time and rediscover the old ways of life that worked. Let's hold onto the good things that keep us healthy like modern dental care and vaccines for the pox, but chuck aside harmful pesticides that are killing the world's bees and genetically modified mutant foods. Progress needs to be redefined using some of the common sense of the gentle farmers of the Shire.

The appendices to *The Lord of the Rings* reveal that after Sam and Rosie Cotton got married they changed their surname. They became "the Gardners," thus starting a long and famous line of Hobbit lads and lassies who worked the ground, making it spring to life in a friendship with the earth.

ChE WISDOM OF ChE ShIRE CELLS US . . .

"To grow your dinner from a seed planted and tended by your own hand is more wondrous than a wizard's sorcery."

Chapter 11

WALK LIKE A HOBBIT

Hobbits love to walk. They'll march from one end of the Shire to the other to steal apples from a particularly good tree or to partake of an excellent beer. It's a good thing they're born with the perfect feet for tromping—big, leathery soles and covered with protective hair—because the heroic Halflings end up walking thousands of miles on their various journeys throughout Middle-earth.✳

Before Frodo sets off to destroy the Ring of Doom, he's become famous in the Shire for his broad wanderings. (He'd learned this love of "tramping" about with his uncle Bilbo when he was a lad.) Frodo would walk far

✳ The actual distance from Hobbiton to Mount Doom (according to *The Atlas of Middle Earth*) was 1,560 miles—several hundred miles farther than the distance from London to Rome.

✳ The stars that Frodo would have seen twinkling in the sky on his night walks in Middle-earth are the same heavenly bodies as in our world's sky, only Tolkien gave them different names. For example, the constellation of Orion's Belt was called "The Swordsman in the Sky."

from home, in woods and hills and under starlight, simply for the joy of wandering. And then the young Hobbit started wondering what lay at the edge of maps, and his explorations took him farther from home. Frodo began dreaming of high mountains—walking had kindled his inner life and desire for adventure.✳

Anyone who has walked around Warwickshire, England, in the glory of summertime knows what the Shire might look like in real life—for this area of England was the childhood inspiration for Tolkien's fantasy world. In "the Heart of England" as it's called, there are public footpaths wending mile after mile through beautiful countryside: on the edges of fields where giant rolls of hay dry in the sun; up hills where lazy ponies munch the grass under ancient oaks; by old crumbling walls of dry-stacked stone; past small copses filled with birdsong and thence into a village with a welcoming pub. That's what one of Frodo's jaunts through his beloved country might have looked like to his Halfling's eyes.

Many physicians agree: walking is one of the healthiest activities for humans. So how come we've all become slaves to our cars? The average American spends nearly an hour in their car to and from work every day. Most healthy people could manage to walk nearly four miles in that amount of time. But it's difficult to walk safely in many areas where sidewalks don't even exist—where pedestrian paths became casualties of urban planning and virtually disappeared from neighborhoods built after World War II. It's one of the reasons Americans feel so vulnerable when we're outside of our powerful engines on wheels.

The Hobbits live in a world that doesn't have cars or trains or ludicrous transportation devices like the Segway. Horses are expensive to keep (even in the Shire) and mainly used for plowing or pulling carts. So the best way to get around is to walk.* It's nothing for a Hobbit to walk fifteen miles or more in a day. Many of us have heard stories from our grandparents about how they had to hoof it several miles in each direction to get to and from school, and they were proud of the fact to boot! Walking great distances used to be the norm in our society.

For Hobbits the act of walking is a sort of art form. They have a style to their outings—a ritual. They usually carry a walk-

* Frodo and his friends (along with Strider) averaged 17.5 miles per day on foot over a period of 28 days on their trek from Hobbiton to Rivendell.

* Before Faramir released Sam and Frodo from Ithilien, he gave each the gift of a walking stick carved from *lebethron*—a wood possessing a kind of magic for "finding and returning." Sam used his to fight off Gollum's sneak attack near Shelob's lair, proving the sticks were also good for hitting.

* This was actually called a "supper-song" in the Shire.

ing stick* with them (good for knocking apples off a high limb or keeping one's balance when scrambling down a craggy hillside) and Tolkien tells us they like to hum when they stroll— usually when they are approaching home after a long day's excursion and are getting excited about the prospects of a warm fire, a good meal and a cozy bed.*

When Frodo, Sam and Pippin are leaving Hobbiton for Crickhollow they hum an ancient "walking-song" that's as "old as the hills." Bilbo had written words for this tune, and Frodo sings it for his friends. The song describes the joys of setting out on a little walking adventure, and the excitement at discovering a beautiful sight in nature no one else has ever beheld before.

The Hobbits are not the only ones who roam around Middle-earth. Aragorn is known to the people of Bree by the name "Strider" because of his vigorous walking habit. The Ranger is perfectly capable of riding, but he goes on foot because he can detect things he would never see if he were on horseback. Everywhere I've traveled in my life

I've kept this notion in mind. When I'm in a big city I go on foot as much as I possibly can.

* The original name for Strider was "Trotter."

I've seen remarkable surprises in big cities like New York, London, Paris and Mumbai that I never would have witnessed had I been in the back of a cab, or on an underground train.*

Walking isn't just an invigorating exercise that's healthy for one's body. It's also a restorative for the mind and soul. When the eight remaining Companions (minus one Balrog-fighting wizard) arrive in Lothlórien after their terrifying ordeal in Moria, one of the things they do to recuperate is to walk amongst the sylvan woods, blissing out on the leaf-strewn paths that wend through the trees. Years before, when Aragorn was a young man, he'd been walking meditatively in these very same woods when he came across the ravishing Arwen Evenstar, also out for a little stroll. It was here that he fell instantly in love with the woman with whom he would eventually plight his troth. You never know what's going to happen when you go for a walk in the woods!

Tom Bombadil is another famous Middle-earth walking fiend. In *The Adventures of Tom Bombadil* he's described as spending his day walking about meadows, playing with bees and "chasing after shadows" in his high-top yellow leather footwear. After Bombadil saves the Hobbits from Old Man Willow, he takes off down the forest path so quickly even the stout-legged Halflings can't keep up with him. And when they awake in the strange man's house the next day, old Traipsing Tom is already back from his predawn hike across the hilltops, like some sort of ultra-marathoner out for his morning workout.

Gandalf is also a great walker. He's known to the Elves as the Grey Wanderer—a renowned and unwearying rambler. Most of the time Gandalf is on foot with his walking staff clutched in one hand. The wizard is, in fact, out for a walk on the day he ambles up to Bilbo's door on that auspicious morning he invites the perplexed Master of Bag End to go on an adventure.

Years later, when Frodo watches Gandalf leave Bag End he muses that although the wizard appears to be a bent old man, he has a surprisingly sturdy gait. Gandalf has kept himself fit for the long centuries he's lived in Middle-earth by exercising his legs. He only tames and rides Shadowfax because he has desperate need of speed.✷

✷ Shadowfax was the chief of the horses of Rohan, who had never let anyone ride him before Gandalf tamed him. He was the strongest, swiftest, and most tireless horse in Middle-earth.

✷ You can visit Ashland, Oregon, home of the Tony Award–winning Shakespeare Festival. Learn more at Ashlandchamber.com.

For years I lived in a town in the foothills of the Siskiyou Mountains of Southern Oregon in a little cottage perched on a hillside. The town is called Ashland,✷ but my friend—a wizardy white-bearded carpenter I worked for—always referred to it as "Hobbiton" because it felt like the Shire. Ashland is located farther from any major metropolitan city than any other small town in America, and so it seemed protected and isolated from the outside world. People living there love to garden, and take long walks in the hills, and eat at one of the hundred or so restaurants in this tourist town (a Hobbit's dream).

Often, I would go an entire week without driving a car in Ashland. I walked there more than I had in my entire life. My wife and parents and I would go on long perambulations nearly every day—step right outside our back door and head up into the hills on the old logging roads above the town, strolling for miles and miles. We felt incredibly healthy and happy. In the recent study of Blue Zones around the world (pockets of civilization where people live to be a hundred years old at ten times the frequency as the United States) walking is one of the keys to longevity. Walking builds bone density and encourages weight loss. It also clears the head.

When Bilbo himself sets out from Bag End for Rivendell in *The Fellowship of the Ring*, he sings "The Road Goes Ever On," a ditty he'd composed upon his return home after the adventure with the Dwarves. He heads to the open road on this new adventure—now unburdened from the Ring—with "eager feet" and a song on his lips. Unless we all want to look like Fatty Bolger (the portliest inhabitant of Hobbiton)

---

* The Proudfoots were a family of Hobbits who enjoyed mispronouncing their names as "Proud*feet*."

we need to stop driving everywhere and get walking like those illustrious Proudfoots of the Shire.*

the wisdom of the shire tells us . . .

"No matter where you live, whether it be city, town or countryside, let your eager feet lead you to wellness, peace of mind and adventure."

Chapter 12

THE GRACE OF THE ELVES

When Gandalf tells Sam he's going to be accompanying Frodo to Rivendell, the young gardener is so excited he bursts into tears. He's like a little kid who's just been told he's going to Disneyland. He's finally going to see a real Elf!

Sam has heard about Elves his entire life. He's grown up at the bottom of the Hill in Hobbiton, practically the next-door neighbor of the famous Mr. Bilbo Baggins, a Hobbit who's actually been to the legendary Rivendell and met the enigmatic ruler of that place—Elrond Half-elven, the son of the legendary mariner Eärendil. Sam has also heard Elven stories and songs, as told by the avuncular Mr. Bilbo.

To Sam, Elves mean *magic*, and that's why he's so excited.

The first time Sam meets one of the Eldar is when the Hobbits are pursued through the Shire by a Ringwraith and, luckily, stumble upon Gildor the Elf walking on a path in the woods. At first the Hobbits hear the Elf lord and his companions singing a song about the Queen of the Stars. And then they see the mysterious Eldar, their bodies shimmering as though radiating a light of their own. Gildor and his friends take the Hobbits into their care for the night and lead them to an Elven campground. They feed the scared and famished Hobbits a delicious meal in the safety of their woodsy hall.

This is one of the hallmarks of the Elves—a profound courtesy for anyone who comes along their path and needs their help. One of their sayings is, "May a star shine on the hour of our meeting."* Frodo knows this saying in Elvish and uses it, much to the happy surprise of Gildor. The greeting means so much more than an obligatory handshake. What you're communicating when you use the salutation of the Elves is a longing for something auspicious: "I hope we become friends, and I hope our friendship lasts."

Frodo learned his modicum of the Elven-tongue from Bilbo who studied the language in earnest after returning home from his adventure with the Dwarves. Why would Bilbo teach his nephew a language Frodo might never use? Hobbits rarely leave the borders of Hobbiton, and Elves hardly ever came into the Shire or interacted

---

* The phrase in the Elven-tongue is "Elen síla lúmenn' omentielvo."

with the Halflings. Perhaps Bilbo simply had a love of the Elves and their lore and wanted to impart that knowledge to Frodo. The stories of the Elves had significance to Bilbo. Their tales stirred his imagination.

Many people, nowadays, wonder what's the use of studying history or ancient languages. What happened in the past (or how people spoke in the past) is useless information to them. Bilbo knew, however, there were important lessons to be learned from the history of his own world. The character of Bilbo is a reflection of his creator, of course. Tolkien was a philologist. He spent his entire career poring over ancient languages (sometimes "dead" ones that were no longer spoken by any living person). But he probably would have never created Middle-earth if it hadn't been for his loving obsession with the words and the mythologies of ancient cultures—an obsession that started for him in childhood.✶

Frodo, fortunate to find himself in the presence of an Elf, begs Gildor's advice about what course of action he should next take. The Elf tells him sagely, "advice is a dangerous gift, even from the wise to the wise." It's a good lesson for anyone. Many of us have given counsel to friends and family—guidance given with the best intentions—only to have it blow up in

✶ Tolkien discovered Finnish as a child and fell in love with it, using it as a model for the Elvish language Quenya. The Elven-tongue Sindarin is based on Old Welsh.

our faces. It's no fun taking the blame for somebody else's problem. But should we simply ignore those who come to us in a time of need, and watch them suffer and brood over an important decision? The answer to that question lies in how much you're willing to get involved. Part of giving that "dangerous gift" of advice is being willing to take the heat for what happens next.

Frodo eventually makes it to Rivendell where Elrond uses all of his powers of healing (including surgery) to cure Frodo of his terrible wound from the Morgul-blade.✷ Frodo wakes up from a coma to find himself in the Last Homely House east of the sea. Over half a century has passed since Bilbo first came here with Gandalf and the Dwarves, but Rivendell hasn't changed at all. It's still a welcoming home—a comforting place filled with food and song and friendly faces. The real magic of the Elves is an intangible force that cures all kinds of woes: "weariness, fear and sadness." The Elves have a capacity for making everything around them better.✷

Have you ever gone to someone's place and instantly felt at home? It might be the first time

✷ The Morgul-blade was the dagger used by the Ringwraith who stabbed Frodo. A splinter of the sinister weapon broke off in the Hobbit's left shoulder and slowly worked its way toward his heart. If it had pierced this vital organ, Frodo would have become a wraith like the Nazgûl.

✷ Rivendell is also known as Imladris in Elven. Both mean "deeply cloven valley."

you've been there, but the moment you walk in the door you feel a release of anxiety, a sense of belonging and happiness. My parents' house is like that. It's one of those places where the door seems to be flying open every few minutes to let some new visitor inside. Guests are greeted with a friendly smile and offered tea or coffee or something homemade to eat. In the winter there's always a fire going, and something tasty cooking on the stove like soup, or cookies baking in the oven. People might be stressed out when they walk up the steps to my mom and dad's house, but when they leave they have smiles on their faces and a boost to their spirits (and some vegetables from my dad's big garden in their arms). They offer friends and strangers a rare kind of civility, and that's just what Rivendell is like.

Does it seem like this kind of Elven courtesy and grace is missing in the world today? Is your home (or even your office) a welcoming kind of place? Do you try to create a friendly atmosphere for your family or coworkers? If not, you might want to ask yourself what is preventing you from doing so. Maybe we should be like the Elven-smiths who wrought the message on the doors to the Mines of Moria. All you have to do is say the word "friend" and the giant magical doors swing right open.*

During the Council of Elrond in Rivendell, representatives from all over

---

* The word "friend" in Elvish is *"mellon."*

* Elrond's ring was called "Vilya"—the Ring of Sapphire, and was once owned by the Elven-king Gil-galad.

Middle-earth come to decide what to do with the One Ring. Elrond, the head of this council, is a paragon of calm strength, and leaders in our world would be wise to study him. His responses are measured but never boring when he explains, several times and emphatically, that Sauron's Ring cannot be used against him. The Elven rings (one of which Elrond wears)* were fashioned for "making, and healing, to preserve all things unstained." But the nature of the One Ring is corrupting. It was made to bring strength to the user and dominion over others. Elrond absolutely fears wielding it.

Elrond uses Saruman the White as an example of a wise and trusted man fallen into depravity. Elrond says it is dangerous to study "the arts of the Enemy too deeply." In the end you will become like the enemy you seek to destroy. Elrond, by the power of his wisdom alone, makes the Council comprehend that the only decision that can be made is to destroy the Ring. He recognizes the strength of will and potential courage in Frodo, even though the Hobbit is small, and deems the task should fall to him. One of the marks of a great leader is the ability to see talents in others.

It's Elrond's idea to put together a Company of Nine Walkers to stand in opposition to the Nine Ringwraiths— the Nazgûl of Sauron. He selects companions for Frodo to represent all of the Free Peoples of Middle-earth. He sends them on their way into the unknown with encouraging words and the advice to not look too far ahead. It's going to be a long road and they need to keep their wits about them and stay in the present.

When the Companions arrive in Lothlórien they are taken to the epicenter of the Golden Wood and presented to Galadriel and her husband. Galadriel has some spooky powers—she can read minds as well as project thoughts into peoples' heads. But each of the Companions (save Boromir who fears her) is enraptured with her regal nature. She is the epitome of urbanity. Even the gruff Gimli is knocked back on his Dwarven heels and falls madly in love.*

The Companions are allowed to rest in Lothlórien and the terrors of Moria quickly vanish in this peaceful and beautiful place. They wander through the sunlit woods, listening to the Elven songs, growing stronger. One day Frodo asks Sam what he thinks of the Elves, and the gardener replies that Galadriel and her people are so completely connected to their surroundings they "seem to belong here, more even than the Hobbits do in the Shire." Theirs is a graceful way of living in harmony with nature that has nearly vanished from our own world.

* Gimli left Middle-earth for the Undying Lands so that he could see Galadriel again. He was the only Dwarf to make this journey.

Everything the Elves do is done with great care and intention, from the "art" of making their sturdy rope to the beautiful tree houses in which they live. Each gift Galadriel bestows upon the Nine Companions is cunningly crafted—the leaf-shaped broaches that fasten their cloaks; the braided belts; and the little box with the gilt lid she gives to Sam.

Galadriel even has grace in defeat. After she rejects Frodo's offer of the Ring of Power—knowing she would eventually become just like Sauron if she were to make use of it—she laughs and speaks in a soft voice, saying she accepts her fate: to diminish and leave Lothlórien forever.

Some of the grace of the Elves rubs off on Frodo. Or perhaps he always had the grace of the Elves, and that was why his uncle wanted him to come live with him in the first place and teach him the Elven language and history. Whatever the case, Faramir recognizes this when he captures Frodo and Sam in the Forest of Ithilien. He tells Frodo he has an "Elvish air" about him. Faramir knows Frodo is going into the darkest, most dangerous place in the world. But the Hobbit has a gravitas that's at odds with his small stature. There's something about Frodo that makes Faramir trust the little Halfling with the peril of "the Ring of Rings," as he calls it.

After the quest is completed, Frodo realizes that his place is no longer in Middle-earth. He lost a piece of his soul in the War of the Ring. He decides to join Gandalf, Bilbo, Galadriel and Elrond on the white ship to Valinor—a journey to the Undying Lands.* He is essentially choosing to die the Elven way. He must say good-bye to everything and everyone he knows and loves.

Most important, he is even saying good-bye to himself.

* The ships going to Valinor made a mystical rather than a maritime journey, passing into another dimension and entering Aman—the Blessed Realm.

* Aragorn, the last of the ancient Númenóreans, had the power to die at will. At the age of 210 he grew weary and gave back "the gift" of life.

In Tolkien's mythology the one god Ilúvatar gives death as a gift to Men. You might be wondering how death can be considered a gift. Wouldn't it be far better to exist as an immortal like the Elves? To live forever without fear of growing old or sick? Death is a terrifying reality—the end of everything.

For Tolkien, Elven immortality comes at a cost. The Elves don't understand the ephemeral nature of life, like we humans (or Hobbits) do. They are resistant to change and attempt to stop time in their havens of Rivendell and Loth-lórien. Without a comprehension of the finite nature of the world, one cannot fully comprehend the gift of life. Every day the cup must be filled to the brim, because it might be your last. And in the end death is the release from the weariness of living too long.*

Tolkien believed the real theme of *The Lord of the Rings*

was the complex notion of "death and the desire for death-lessness." The Men (and Hobbits) are doomed to die and leave Middle-earth for the unknown. The Elves are also doomed to leave Middle-earth and return to the Undying Lands, where they are subject to the gods and no longer masters of themselves and their world. They must "diminish" as Galadriel says after her temptation of the Ring and bow to powerful godlike entities—the Valar.

The Elves finally accept their great change—their giving up of Middle-earth—with the grace of their kind, just like we must someday face the unavoidable exit from our world. Sometimes we witness the old or terminally ill facing the prospect of death with a beautiful resignation. Others fight the great change, resisting until the very end. The white ship leaving the Grey Havens with its fatalistic passengers is a metaphor of accepting the end of one life, and moving on to another phase of existence.

the wisdom of the shire tells us . . .

"May the grace of the Elves teach you courtesy, a love of learning, calm-strength and acceptance."

Chapter 13

LOVE IN THE THIRD AGE

Tolkien has been criticized by some pundits for the scarcity of bodice ripping in his books. We must remember, however, that the master of Middle-earth was a product of the Victorian age, when a man could be brought to trial for lewd behavior simply by gesturing toward a young lady with the wrong end of his badminton racket.*

Tolkien's work is entirely bereft of the risqué. The naughty bits in *The Lord of the Rings* are tucked away in the appendices, and it is here we may uncover the romantic exploits of the Shire or *coHobbitations* of the agrarian Halflings

---

* Tolkien was born in 1892, a year before G. B. Shaw's shocking play about a female brothel owner (*Mrs. Warren's Profession*) was banned from the theatre. It wasn't performed until Tolkien was twenty-three years old and engaged to be married.

who live in the so-called Third Age of Middle-earth. Farmers, as everyone knows, like to get down and dirty— and not just in the garden. According to Tolkien's racy back matter, Sam Gamgee and his wife Rosie had thirteen children! Now we really know what was going on in those Hobbit-holes.*

Merry is referred to as Meriadoc "the Magnificent" and yet he remained childless, probably from the effects of too much Ent-water and Longbottom Leaf. The more likely answer, though, is that spending all those days tucked into the saddle nestled against the bosom of the fair Lady Éowyn of Rohan spoiled him forever and turned him cold to Shire lassies.* Pippin, always the rascal, married a woman scandalously named Diamond of Long Cleve (*cleve* being the Saxon word for "bedchamber").

The most lovelorn inhabitants in Middle-earth are the sad old Ents who drifted apart from the females of their species. The Entwives wanted to settle down and start gardens and grow things. The males didn't want to put down roots— they had a wanderlust to explore new lands, and so they left their womenfolk behind.

* The names of Sam and Rosie's children were, in order of birth: Elanor, Frodo, Rose, Merry, Pippin, Goldilocks, Hamfast, Daisy, Primrose, Bilbo, Ruby, Robin, and Tolman (Tom).

* Merry spent six full days in the saddle with Éowyn, who was riding disguised as a man and going under the alias "Dernhelm" (which translates as "Secret Helm").

And then tragedy struck the tree people. War ravaged the land of the Entwives and when the Ents returned to their women all they found were burned and barren fields and rumors of a diaspora. No matter where the Ents searched they could not find their Entwives. Treebeard is like some sad old man lamenting the girl who got away. The Ents had their magical water, but it was nothing compared to the elixir of love, even if the woman you pine for might, in fact, be *made* of pine!

But at least the Ents were yearning for something lost. The Dwarves of Middle-earth seem to have never had any love life at all. The appendices to *The Lord of the Rings* also tells us that there was only one female Dwarf to every three males. And they looked so much like their counterparts they were nearly impossible to tell apart. Gimli, therefore, must be an aberration of his race. He is so utterly smitten by the Elven Lady Galadriel that he begs to be given a strand of her golden tresses that he might encase it in crystal and thus keep as an heirloom of his house. Later on in the tale Galadriel teasingly sends a message to Gimli referring to the Dwarf as her "Lockbearer," causing the Dwarf to go into an ax-swinging rapture.

Critics who insist Tolkien was uninterested in romance need only look to his own life to contradict these claims. He was married to his soul mate Edith for fifty-five years (until she passed away). In *The Lord of the Rings*

Aragorn and Arwen share a similar heroic monogamy. They are plighted in troth for sixty-seven years. This is, without a doubt, the longest engagement in the history of literature.

It's pretty hard to get hitched, however, when your father-in-law (Elrond: half-elven, full-on somber) demands that before you marry you must succeed in destroying the armies of the Dark Lord of Mordor, then become King of Gondor *and* Arnor.

Aragorn fell in love with Arwen at first sight. He saw her walking through the woods of Rivendell and called out to her "Tinúviel! Tinúviel!" which is the Elven equivalent of shouting, "By the Heathen Kings of Old that's one stunning Elf-maid!"* Just before Aragorn saw Arwen he had been daydreaming about Beren and Lúthien—Middle-earth's most romantic duo. These two shared a love so profound their story makes the tragedy of Romeo and Juliet look like Mickey and Minnie Mouse in comparison.

Lúthien's father would only allow Beren to marry his daughter if the young warrior managed to cut one of the fabulous Silmaril jewels from the crown of Morgoth—a virtually impossible task. For Morgoth was a creature so evil he made his nasty servant Sauron look about as scary as one of the Sackville-Bagginses.

Lúthien saved Beren from a hellish dungeon, sucked poison from his wounds and performed a torch song for that dirty old reprobate Morgoth, singing him to sleep so Beren could cut the Silmaril from his iron crown. Beren, for his part, took an arrow for Lúthien, and lost his hand protecting her from Morgoth's pet werewolf.

And all of this so they could get married.

When Beren died from wounds he suffered fighting the wolf-beast a second time, Lúthien passed away on the spot from grief. Her spirit journeyed to the kingdom of Mandos—the Judge of the Dead. Mandos thought her voice was so beautiful he decided to bring Beren and Lúthien back to life!

Aragorn, using this unprecedented romance as a guide for his love for Arwen Evenstar, remains faithful to his Elven Lady even when Éowyn, shieldmaiden of Rohan, makes it known (with many longing looks) that she would let him "take her to the stables" of Edoras. Aragorn snubs her, though. He's got a Minas Tirith marriage on the mind.*

Tolkien's heroes, you see, were monogamous heroes. The paragons of true love in Middle-earth must go through terrible ordeals before they can find happiness. True love for them is like the shards of Narsil reforged in a fiery furnace—the hammer blows only

* Aragorn and Arwen were married on Midsummer Day and their marital bliss lasted for 6 score years (or 120 years) until Aragorn's death. Their son was named Eldarion.

make it all the stronger. How many of us have given up on a relationship simply because of some minor impediment or perceived fault in our partner? Tolkien's lovers have the hearts and determination of warriors who stay true despite separation, loneliness and temptation.

I fell in love my first day of college. The instant I saw her I knew the same crazy joy that Beren felt when he saw Lúthien in the Elven glade, or Aragorn when he caught sight of Arwen, or when Sam Gamgee first spotted Rosie Cotton.

One of the first things my girlfriend and I did together was read *The Lord of the Rings* out loud to each other in our dorm rooms. And if you're thinking we were a couple of innocent dorks, you're right. But it seems like innocence is on the wane these days. Wouldn't you like some of it back in your own life? I know I would.

There is another love story in *The Lord of the Rings* that is just as profound as Beren and Lúthien or Arwen and Aragorn. And that's the platonic love Sam has for Frodo. He is willing to sacrifice everything to stay with his friend, and even give up his own life to help him in his quest—to help him destroy the terrible burden of the Ring.

Sam's love is mightier than the Ring of Doom and it gives him the strength to face seemingly insurmountable odds including single-handedly storming a tower full of maniacal Orcs, and facing down one very scary little Ring-obsessed lunatic.

Love, as they say, will make you do some crazy things.

So why is it so difficult for us to find true and lasting love like Tolkien and his creations—Beren, Aragorn and Sam? And if we are married, why is it so hard to keep from growing bored with our partners . . . to remain faithful? Has the act of marriage become another casualty of our epoch: the Disposable Age? Why can't we be like Tom Bombadil and his bride Goldberry, shacked up like a couple of groovy hippies since the Dawn of Time, eating and making love and skinny-dipping in the River Withywindle singing "Come merry-dol!"✳

Perhaps we've become too jaded or too picky or just too lazy to try and make love last. We look to celebrity couples for our exemplars of marital bliss, and then shake our heads in dismay when their relationships fall apart over infidelity or boredom. Maybe we should look to the life of Tolkien himself as an exemplar of love.

Tolkien met Edith when he was sixteen and still in school. They were forced to stay apart by Tolkien's guardian because of their religious differences (he was a Catholic, she a Protestant). But Tolkien never gave up hope he would be with her. When he came of age he begged her to marry him. They were engaged for three long years, and were finally wed

✳ Tom Bombadil and Goldberry were immortals and possibly the oldest living entities in Middle-earth other than Sauron. Their marriage, therefore, was the longest in the history of that world.

* Sam's daughter, Rosie, grew up to marry Pippin's son, Faramir, named in honor of his Gondorian friend.

on the eve of WWI. Less than three months later Tolkien was serving on the Western Front, while Edith waited home, agonizing that he would be killed. But they survived all of these trials and lived a long and happy life together, raising a family.

I think one of the most amazing things about *The Lord of the Rings* is that it's an epic adventure with titanic sieges and demonic wraiths and evil sorcerers and armies of ghosts and mighty talking battle trees, and yet it ends with a guy coming home to his little house and putting his daughter on his knee and letting out a great big sigh.

"Well, I'm back," says Sam. It's the final line of the book.*

For many years after college my Tolkien-loving girl-friend and I had to live apart, separated by thousands of miles and sometimes by entire oceans, but we remained faithful, hoping that someday we would be together—knowing it would only come to pass if we stayed true. Now, like Sam, I have my own daughter and son to hold, and I know a truth about life: a happy child on your knee is more powerful than any magic in Middle-earth. I'm still in love with that girl I met in college. I'm just lucky she decided to marry me . . . after a *very* long engagement.

Tolkien died less than two years after his wife and

asked to be buried in the same grave. On their tombstones, below their Christian names, he ordered their pet names to be carved: BEREN AND LÚTHIEN. He'd spent over half a century in love with the same woman. And he probably hoped, like the characters from his story, he and his wife would get a second chance to be together, even after death.✳

✳ You can pay your respects to J.R.R. Tolkien's grave at Wolvercote Cemetery in North Oxford. This is what appears on the tombstone:

EDITH MARY TOLKIEN
LÚTHIEN
1889–1971
JOHN RONALD
REUEL TOLKIEN
BEREN
1892–1973

The Wisdom of the Shire Tells Us . . .

"True love must be defended bravely with the soul of a warrior, and yet tended with the patience of a gardener."

Chapter 14

THE FELLOWSHIP
OF THE SHIRE

There's a special camaraderie amongst the inhabitants of the Shire that goes beyond mere friendship. Frodo and his friends are a "fellowship" long before the Nine Companions set out from Rivendell. The Hobbits share a bond that will not be broken and they're exemplars of the motto, "A friend in need is a friend indeed."＊

Hobbits will scuffle over a plate of sautéed mushrooms, of course, but they'll lay down their lives to save someone they love as Merry demonstrates when he attacks the Witch-king of Angmar to protect Éowyn; and Pippin when he races through the war-torn streets of Minas Tirith to alert Gandalf about Faramir's premature funeral pyre arrangement;

＊ At the start of *The Lord of the Rings,* Frodo was 50 years old, Merry 36, Sam 35, and Pippin 28.

or Sam when he fights the monstrous spider Shelob.*

We first catch a glimpse of the steadfastness of the Halflings in *The Hobbit* when Thorin and the Dwarves are caught by the giant spiders of Mirkwood and wrapped up in cocoons. Bilbo has every reason to turn and run from this terrible nest of overgrown arachnids, but he isn't going to let his friends get turned into juice for spiders. His courage to attack the monsters is admirable. But it's his loyalty to his friends that spurs him to bravery.

* Shelob was Sauron's wicked pet. The Dark Lord sent live prisoners to her as food. The disgusting arachnid was about as close as Gollum had to a friend.

* Because Pippin was under thirty-three he was still considered—by the standards of the Shire—to be an underage "tween."

Merry and Pippin are examples of persistency in friendship too. They know Frodo is planning to leave Hobbiton on some mission of danger, and so they plot in secret to go along with him no matter what, "through thick and thin—to the bitter end" as they tell him. And in Rivendell Pippin declares that Elrond will have to tie him up and send him back to the Shire in a sack if he won't let him go with his friends on the rest of the journey. At certain points in the journey Gandalf probably wishes Elrond had taken the young Took up on his threat.*

Sam is the paragon of this indefatigable friendship. He journeys with Frodo into the hell of Mordor, knowing full well the dangers, and eventually realizes there will be no coming back to the Shire. But even then he refuses to give up heart. He's constantly trying to cheer up Frodo, never giving in to the despair or darkness of their seemingly impossible task. Whenever he can he steers Frodo's morbid thoughts back toward the light of the Shire—the origin of their deep bond.

The Hobbits are relentless in a good way. They stick like glue to their friends. After Frodo is stabbed by the Ringwraith and ends up in a coma in the House of Elrond, Sam stays by his bedside for nearly four days and nights, watching over him. And when Merry is lost amongst the dead after the Battle of Pelennor Fields, Pippin searches nonstop until he finds his shell-shocked friend and brings him to the Houses of Healing in Minas Tirith.

Good friends help you through illness and bad times, and they don't let you fall through the cracks, no matter what kind of problems you're facing. It seems like it's getting harder and harder nowadays to have close friends like these, doesn't it? Everyone is busy to the point of madness with barely enough time to socialize unless it's via postings on Facebook where "I'm eating a sandwich" apparently qualifies as an Internet version of a conversational gambit.

Staying close to old friends from childhood or college is

made more difficult (and sometimes impossible) when we're spread all over the planet with our various global careers. So what was it about the Hobbits that made them so truehearted toward their friends? And how did they keep that connection for their entire lives?

To answer these questions it might be helpful to explore the roots of a Hobbit's upbringing in the Shire—Frodo in particular. After his parents died in a boating accident he went to live with his late mother's relatives at Brandybuck Hall. The Gaffer describes the place as a regular "warren" and we can easily imagine the young Frodo in a rambling tunnel-filled Hobbit-hole teeming with rambunctious cousins. If Merry Brandybuck is any indication of the character of his family they are a breed of happy, fun-loving, candid, quick-witted and dependable Hobbits.

Buckland and the neighboring Shire would have been like gigantic playgrounds for Frodo and his companions, with wide-open fields to run through, rivers to swim,* and little woods to explore. Frodo was, by several accounts, quite the young imp. We know he was chased out of Farmer Maggot's farm for stealing mushrooms, and there's no doubt he got his love of traipsing about the countryside in the early days of his youth.

Frodo is eventually brought to Bag End where his kindly un-

---

* Only the Hobbits of Buckland learned to swim and operate boats.

cle Bilbo makes him his heir, probably because he recognized his own
adventurous nature in Frodo. Here
Bilbo teaches Frodo a smattering of
Elven-tongue and poetry, and a love of lore and maps. But
even with this "higher education"* and the trappings of
wealth Frodo fits right in with the simple agrarian society
of Hobbiton. There are rich people like Bilbo and the
Brandybucks, of course, but there is no aristocracy or ruling class. Sam might call Frodo "master" but they are
equals as Hobbits. Can you imagine Lord Crowley of
Downton Abbey knocking back a few pints and belting
out a drinking song with *his* gardener?

As an adult, Frodo and his childhood friends have a
merry time with one another, joking and singing and
telling stories, drinking beer and going on long walks.
They like to take the piss out of each other—to give
each other a gentle roasting. And they possess a healthy
dose of self-effacing humor. It's easy to be friends with
people who are cheerful and don't take themselves too
seriously. And friendship comes easy when your friends
don't want anything more from you than the joy of your
company.

The Hobbits have time to cultivate friendships—vast
amounts of time to just hang out and simply be together.
In a way they have lower expectations about how their
friends should act than we do. We have so little time to be

with our friends in this hectic world that when we can get together it usually has to be while doing something *amazing*. There's so much pressure we end up acting like performers. We have to be witty, charming, interesting and interested. We can't just sit around and eat a meal or go for a walk. Instead we have to be in a book club, or take part in an epic and expensive ski trip, or help build a mechanical float and head to Burning Man. It's all so exhausting being friends in this era. There's so much less pressure when you're just Hobbitting about.

One of the best personality traits of the Hobbits is that they have the innocence of children without being childish. The fierce King Théoden—who meets Merry and Pippin soon after the dreadful Battle of the Hornburg—can't help but forget the dire circumstances of the War of the Ring and banters with the amusing "Holbytlan" as he calls them. Gandalf warns Théoden not to encourage them. They'll make small talk on the "edge of ruin" says the wizard in his gruff way. (But you know that Gandalf loves them too.)*

What Gandalf is really saying about the Hobbits is that they are undaunted. They may not have the innate bravery of Aragorn or Boromir, but they refuse to be downcast, even in the

* Gandalf had been watching out for his beloved Shire-folk for centuries. Almost two hundred years before the events of the War of the Ring he came to the aid of Hobbits during a terrible and deadly winter.

face of disaster or death. Perhaps Gandalf instinctively knew to send Bilbo along with Thorin & Co. because he realized the good-natured Hobbit would be a healthy dose of amiability amongst the surly Dwarves. It's Bilbo's desire to save his friends from certain death that leads him to steal the Arkenstone and give it to the Elven-king, thus incurring Thorin's murderous wrath. But in the end, the Dwarf and Hobbit make up as friends, even if it is on Thorin's deathbed.

If you've ever had a falling out with a good friend or family member in your life, the death of Thorin scene from *The Hobbit* has a particular resonance. It's very difficult for us to swallow our pride and either ask for forgiveness or accept it from somebody else when they ask it of us. Human nature is such that we feel the most pain from a perceived betrayal when the person who perpetrated the wrong against us was someone we trusted or thought of as a close friend. If Bilbo can rekindle a bond with a comrade who called him a rat and was about to throw him to his death off a high wall, you can renew a friendship with someone who hurt your feelings.

In *The Return of the King*, Sam shows an amazing capacity for forgiveness. After rescuing Frodo from the tower of Cirith Ungol, Frodo is seized by the madness of the Ring and lets forth a venomous rant at his friend, accusing him of trying to steal his Ring. When Frodo comes to his senses he apologizes, and Sam merely wipes his tears on his sleeve and forgives his friend. Later, when Frodo is utterly exhausted and can't move an inch farther, Sam hoists Frodo onto his back and carries him as though he were giving a child a piggyback ride—albeit a ride up the flinty slopes of Orodruin.*

After the Hobbits drive out the Shire invaders at the end of *The Return of the King*, they settle down to a quiet life. Sam marries Rosie and they move into Bag End where they take care of Frodo who is suffering from his old wounds (both physical and psychological). He's like a WWI veteran recovering from trench fever. But Frodo feels lucky. He knows there's not a Hobbit in the Shire who's being looked after with such care.

. Merry and Pippin spend their days after the War of the Ring "cutting a dash" around the countryside, singing and laughing and telling fine tales. But most of all they become famous for their "excellent parties." In the end perhaps the greatest threat to the evil of Sauron was not men at arms, but rather the bonds of love that kept the Hobbits from letting their friends fall into darkness and despair.*

---

* Orodruin: the Elvish word for Mount Doom meaning "fiery-mountain."

* Merry and Pippin traveled to Gondor to be with their friend Aragorn just before they both died. They were buried in "beds" or tombs that were set on either side of the King's final resting place in the new burial chamber of Minas Tirith, the old chamber having been burned down by the mad Denethor.

ᴄhe wisᴅoᴍ of ᴄhe shiʀe ᴄells us . . .

"May a star shine on the hour of your meeting a new friend, and continue to light up the long path of your friendship."

Chapter 15

THE PARTY TREE

The "Party Tree" was the gigantic tree that grew just south of Bag End and was the site of Bilbo's famous eleventy-first birthday party, where hundreds of families from around the Shire came to share in his and his nephew Frodo's combined celebration.

The tree was a magnificent specimen, thick of trunk and vivid with autumn leaves, a colorful symbol of Bilbo's lofty standing in the Shire. A giant tent was erected over the Party Tree, enclosing it in a canvas pavilion, and lanterns were hung from the limbs. It was underneath this tree that Bilbo gave his famous Farewell Speech, before slipping on the One Ring and disappearing from the Shire forever.*

* At the end of *The Lord of the Rings,* Bilbo is one hundred and thirty-one years old, having lived to see one more birthday than the famous Old Took.

* The Two Trees of Valinor lit up the world at the start of creation. After the trees were wantonly destroyed by the wicked demigod Melkor, the gods made the sun and moon as gifts to give light to the inhabitants of Middle-earth.

* Galadriel's power came from her magical ring Nenya, a gift she received from the Elven smith Celebrimbor; its strength was bound to the One Ring.

When Frodo and his friends return to Bag End after the War of the Ring, they are stunned to see the Party Tree has been chopped down and is now rotting in the field. This was one of Saruman the wizard's final malicious acts, like Melkor cutting down the Two Trees of Valinor.* Saruman wanted to kill all joy in Hobbiton. Destroying the symbol of birthdays was the most obvious thing for him to do.

Sam is so overcome with emotion he bursts into tears. In his eyes this is worse than the desolation of Mordor. But Sam bucks up and quickly replants the tree with the single silver seed given to him by Galadriel.*

Birthdays are very important to the Hobbits, you must understand. And they have a unique way of celebrating them. Instead of *getting* presents, they *give* them. Every day of the year, we're told, it's probably someone's birthday in the Shire, and so a Hobbit is likely to get a present every day of the year. This is one of their little ways of reaffirming life.

Hobbits don't give big gifts, mind you. Instead they re-gift little presents called *mathoms*—things that are lying around their own cluttered Hobbit-hole. The origin of the word comes from the Old English name for a treasure that was presented to a warrior in payment for a great deed in battle. In the olden days of the Shire, long before the War of the Ring begins, the Hobbits had to fight for survival in a dangerous world. At the start of *The Lord of the Rings*, however, all of the ancient trophies of war are collecting dust in Mathom-house (the Shire's equivalent of a museum).

In this age of Middle-earth a *mathom* for a Hobbit might be food or something useful like clothing. Gifting has become a symbol of friendship rather than the glory of war. Gollum, when he claims to have been given the One Ring as a birthday present, is perverting the sanctity of this Hobbit act of generosity.

Bilbo's eleventy-first birthday party was a grand event, with singing and dancing, enough food to feed practically the entire Shire, as well as games and fireworks. Anyone who's seen the film adaptation of *The Fellowship of the Ring* knows what a Hobbit celebration probably looks like. But what about a smaller, more intimate party?*

Let's imagine a young Hobbit's birthday party five years after Bilbo's epic shindig. He's invited a few of his closest friends to his

* Frodo continued the tradition of celebrating his own and Bilbo's birthdays (without the presence of his favorite uncle, of course) every season in the years following the great eleventy-first birthday.

comfortable hole in the bank of a hill. It's September (the month of *Halimath* by "*Shire-reckoning*"). The guests start arriving around sundown and are greeted at the door by their smiling host. The gardener is first, straight from washing up after a hard but happy day's work.

Then comes a very portly fellow, famous in the Shire for his girth, and eager for dinner to start. He hangs up his colorful cloak on a peg in the hall and turns as "the cousins" burst through the door, a drinking-song on their lips. They're a notorious pair of mischief-makers who've come straight from The Ivy Bush where they've been sampling the new ale.

Soon it's "raining food and snowing drink" as the old Hobbit saying goes. The friends feast and drink, and sing about feasting and drinking, starting off the night with "The Man in the Moon Stayed Up Too Late" and going straight into "The Man in the Moon Came Down Too Soon." And then doing them both again for good measure.

After they've stuffed themselves on Hobbit fare, and have a playful shoving match to see who gets the last stuffed mushroom, they break out the Longbottom Leaf and the host starts passing around the presents—a special gift for each of his friends. Some pruning shears for his gardener, travel-sized pipes for the cousins, a walking stick for his portly friend (to encourage a little exercise).

The young Hobbit's guests praise him to the top of the Party Tree. Then to the moon! Nay! To the Star of Eärendil shining so brightly in the sky! They take a walk together under the stars, breathing in the crisp night air, and wonder what lies beyond the distant hills, far to the east where lies adventure and the unknown.✴

* After the Ring had been destroyed the Hobbits celebrated Bilbo's one hundred and twenty-ninth birthday with him in Rivendell. Bilbo gave Frodo three books of lore he'd written titled *Translations from the Elvish, by B.B.*

When I was in my early twenties I decided to have a Hobbit birthday. I was very poor at the time, practically destitute, and so I gave my friends and family *mathoms*— books and CDs and things I had on hand. I asked everyone to refrain from giving me gifts as part of my experiment. It actually felt better giving than getting, despite the many things I could have used. It was a liberating event.

In this age of conspicuous consumption and mass consumerism, is it really necessary for adults to have birthday parties every year where they are lavished with gifts? Advertisers distort reality so thoroughly they'd have us believe the only gift that could truly make us happy (and satisfy that emptiness in our souls) is a new car, or perhaps a diamond ring. Wouldn't it be an interesting change to have a Hobbit birthday?

Lembas, the nourishing waybread of the Elves given to the Companions, was wrapped in the leaves of *mallorn* trees to keep it fresh.

Here's what you might try. On the illustrious day of your birth try giving presents to all of your family and friends. You can make the presents yourself, or just offer them some little *mathom* that's lying around your house—something you love like a book or an object you've picked up in your travels. Then cook a Hobbit feast and invite everyone you love for a celebration not only of your life, but also of your life *with* them.

The Lady Galadriel doesn't need the excuse of a birthday to bestow gifts upon the Companions. Upon their departure from Lothlórien she provides them all with something from her stockpile of Elven *mathoms*: a sheath, a broach, a bow and quiver, belts and some strands of her hair (for a besotted Dwarf). To Frodo she bestows a crystal phial containing the magical light of Eärendil. And to Sam she gives the most magical gift of all—that small wooden box filled with the dust of the Golden Wood and a single *mallorn* seed.*

Perhaps Galadriel foresaw the destruction of the Party Tree in her mystical mirror. Maybe she knew that nothing she could ever give to Sam would mean more than the resurrection of the symbol of Hobbiton. Sam lives a long and happy life after the War of the Ring. Frodo gives him and his wife Bag End where they raise thirteen children. The new Party Tree, we must assume, becomes an enormous and famous landmark, towering above the Hill.*

* The new Party Tree was the only Elven *mallorn* tree to grow west of the Misty Mountains.

After Sam's wife Rosie dies decades later, the grief-stricken Hobbit departs the Shire forever and heads to the Grey Havens where he will sail over the sea to the Undying Lands, the last of the Ring-bearers. The date is September 22nd. The shared birthday of his beloved friends—Frodo and Bilbo.

The Wisdom of the Shire Tells Us . . .

"Celebrate your birthday by honoring others with the mathom *of your friendship and love."*

Chapter 16

SING LIKE A HOBBIT

The Lord of the Rings could easily be turned into a Broadway musical because nearly every inhabitant of Middle-earth bursts into song at the drop of a hat, from our favorite lay-singing Ranger to a chanting Barrow-wight to a chorus of long-limbed Ents. The only creatures that don't sing are the Orcs (who would probably scream heavy metal if they could).*

Hobbits, however, are the most prodigious singers. And they love to sing about the fun they're having *while* they're having it. They'll join in a "walking song" while they're out for a stroll, or croon a "bathing song" while scrubbing their wooly feet, or belt out a "drinking song" while

---

* Several heavy metal bands have taken their names from *The Lord of the Rings*, including Gorgoroth and Burzum (both words from the language of Mordor).

guzzling beer. They want to express their joy for life, and one of the ways they do that is with song.

The importance of song in Tolkien's works is sometimes overlooked. *The Silmarillion*—the mythological underpinning of Middle-earth—begins with a cosmic melody. Heavenly spirits called the Ainur, the first creations of the god Ilúvatar, intone together in beautiful harmony, filling the Void with their music. But the demigod Melkor, the most powerful amongst these entities, doesn't want to play along with the others, and creates a discordant music of his own, drowning out the others and silencing them. He ends up in a musical showdown with Ilúvatar—sort of like "dueling banjos" across the vaults of heaven.

In *The Hobbit* Bilbo is bewitched by a Dwarven song, and it's one of the main reasons he heads off on the adventure to the Lonely Mountain. You wouldn't think a bunch of tough-as-iron Dwarves would be musicians. But Thorin and his followers show up at Bag End with their own musical instruments in velvet bags: harps, fiddles and flutes. Imagine a bunch of murderous-looking Hell's Angels taking over your house and then breaking out into folk songs!

The Dwarves chant a haunting hymn of the Lonely Mountain—a poetic tale of gleaming gold and shimmering jewels and a rampaging dragon. A dormant part of Bilbo suddenly flames up inside him and he realizes he wants to "wear a sword instead of a walking stick." That night he falls asleep with the Dwarven music still in his ears—a song that has more power to entangle the Hobbit's soul than any wizard's spell. His dreams are "uncomfortable," meaning they're filled with a yearning that goes beyond his simple life in the Shire.

We've all had an experience like this. With me it was U2's *The Unforgettable Fire*, an album that was so completely different from anything I had ever heard up until that point in my life. It blew me away. That record was full of stories: civil rights and the majesty of nature and tempestuous love and addiction. Even the title had meaning—it was a reference to the horrors of Hiroshima. The lyrics spoke to my teenage heart. This was poetry. It made me want to read books, and venture out into the world, and discover something about myself. When was the last time music did that for you?∗

Bilbo doesn't have much to sing about on the trip to the Lonely Mountain, and the Dwarves never play their instruments again. But this Hobbit, who didn't have a shred of poetry in him before setting out on his adventure, comes home with poetry in his soul. As he and Gandalf are heading back into the Shire, Bilbo starts reciting his famous "The Road Goes Ever On."

Whenever I come back

∗ Tolkien's *The Adventures of Tom Bombadil* contains songs and poems supposedly written by Bilbo and Sam (including one called "Oliphaunt," most likely penned by that courageous elephant-loving gardener).

from a trip—especially if I've traveled far and been gone a long time—I hear those words in my head. This song has some of the greatest lyrics ever written about the allure of the road.

✶ In the film version of *The Fellowship of the Ring*, the first time we see Gandalf he's humming "The Road Goes Ever On" as he drives his fireworks-laden cart down the wooded lane towards Hobbiton.

It's about wanderlust, but it's also about the joy of coming back home. On a deeper level it can be taken as a song about death and the journey of the soul, going on and on even after this life is done. A prim and proper Hobbit goes away with the Dwarves, but a troubadour returns to Bag End. Bilbo spends the rest of his life composing songs and poems.✶

When I was twenty-two I literally lost the ability to speak or sing. I had to have a painful reconstructive surgery on my face to correct a genetic defect, and it took me about a year to teach myself how to use my mouth and jaw again. For months I was practically mute. My face was so altered I didn't even recognize myself in a mirror, and friends I'd known my entire life passed me on the street without knowing who I was.

One of the things that kept me sane during this dark time was *The Lord of the Rings*. I read it over and over again for comfort. To forget about the agony and the humiliation that went along with this temporary disfigurement. Reading Tolkien was like hanging out with an old friend and having a joyful conversation—a conversation I couldn't have in real life.

Since that experience I've never taken for granted my ability to communicate, and I have empathy for people who are afraid to speak up or let their voices ring out. We are interactive creatures, and one of the most profound ways we express our thoughts and emotions is through song.

Is music an important part of your life? Most of us listen to music, of course, or watch some variant of the "root out the next pop star!" TV shows. But do you actually sing yourself? And have you ever wanted to learn to play an instrument like a guitar or a ukulele? Because I'm here to tell you you're never too old to pick them up. I didn't learn to play those two instruments until I was well into my thirties, and since then some of the most fun times I've ever had with family and friends have been sitting around playing music together. It's remarkable how a bunch of Americans can sing a uniquely Australian song like "Waltzing Matilda," while understanding very little of the strange words, yet connecting to the heart and soul of the song in a powerful way.*

* The actor Billy Boyd (who played Pippin Took in Peter Jackson's film trilogy) is lead singer and guitarist in an alternative rock band based in Glasgow, Scotland, called Beecake. (beecake.com)

The Hobbits aren't worried if their voices are up to anybody's standards, and that's one of the reasons they feel such freedom to sing. They just pipe away to their heart's content. Sometimes, however, they give voice to song when they're terrified and alone. When Sam is sitting outside the Tower of Cirith Ungol, utterly at the end of his rope, he starts to sing in a "thin and quavering" voice some tunes from his childhood, with snippets of Bilbo's lyrics he's heard over the years. And then his voice grows stronger, and all of a sudden he rings out with a fully formed song that's all about hope and the coming of spring. It's his way of defying the darkness of Mordor. It's his "Somewhere Over the Rainbow."

Aragorn is connected to music in a way that is almost mystical. When he and the Hobbits are hiding out from the Ringwraiths on Weathertop, he sings to the Shire-folk "the Lay of Leithian"—the ancient love story of Beren and Lúthien. The song mirrors the Ranger's own story of a mortal falling in love with an Elf. For Aragorn, however, it's more than just a tale from days gone by. The lay links him to his own history and gives meaning to his life in the present in the same way folk songs do for people around the world.

Bilbo and Aragorn become friends when the Hobbit moves to Rivendell. The Ranger collaborates with the Shire poet and they work on an epic about Eärendil the

✳ The Beatles had the idea to create what would have been the first film version of *The Lord of the Rings* with George as Gandalf, Paul as Frodo, Ringo as Sam and John as Gollum.

✳ Bret McKenzie, who played the Elf Figwit in *The Lord of the Rings* and the Elf Lindir in *The Hobbit* films, wrote "Life's a Happy Song" (for which he won an Academy Award).

Mariner. Bilbo loves grand tales of the Elves and the earlier ages, but he's also capable of writing introspective and unpretentious works, like the short unnamed song he sings to Frodo about death and what the world will be like when he's gone. It's Bilbo's "Yesterday."✳

There's one character in *The Lord of the Rings* whose life is practically a nonstop musical—and that's Tom Bombadil. He sings about himself, and about the woods and river and starlight and his beautiful wife Goldberry. You can just imagine him breaking into "Life's a Happy Song" and all the trees and animals of the Old Forest coming to life and singing along.✳

Tom Bombadil also uses his songs to cast spells. When the Hobbits end up inside the tree-trap of Old Man Willow, Tom sings them out of their predicament. Tom's words are magic, and Frodo later uses his lyrics to call for help when his friends are captured by the Barrow-wight—a creature who just happens to be a singing ghoul!

After the Companions lose Gandalf in Moria, they find a haven in Lothlórien and take respite there, listening to the

sounds of Elves singing lamenta-
tions to Mithrandir (the Elvish
name for the wizard). The Hobbits can't understand the "sweet
sad words" of the Elves, but they
are touched to their hearts. This is something the Hobbits
comprehend completely—the inexplicable expression of
emotion with song. The Elves inspire Frodo and Sam to
come up with their own spoken memorials for Gandalf.✶

✶ The new age group
Shadowfax took their
name from the horse
Gandalf "borrowed" from
the Rohirrim.

Even Galadriel is a songstress. When the Companions
leave Lothlórien she sings them a farewell song while playing the harp. One can imagine her "sweet" voice weaving
a melancholy tale of the end of her Elven kingdom and the
departure of her kind from Middle-earth. It's Galadriel's
version of "I Dreamed a Dream."

I've heard people say a particular artist or type of music
has been "the soundtrack of my life." For some people it's
Nirvana, for others it's Broadway show tunes. I'm always
amazed how a song heard on the radio can take me back to
a moment in my life with the power of a time machine.
Whenever I hear The Beatles' "Here Comes the Sun" on the
radio I'm instantly transported back forty years to one of my
earliest memories—listening to that song on the car radio
with my mom singing along with her lovely voice. That's
magic.

Nowadays it seems like the music industry has taken

commercialization to a whole new level of corporate control and greed. Companies can track your likes and dislikes on the Internet and even get access to what you buy and how often. I have no doubt that someday they'll figure out a way to create synthetic "artists" tailor-made for customers. There will be no more human connection to music and the people who make it.

I have a solution to part of this problem. Start making your *own* music. Create the soundtrack to your life. If you have children, sing to them and sing *with* them as much and as often as you can. Make and invent and play your own music, just like the folk of the Shire would do. Have your friends come over and teach each other songs. Buy yourself a ukulele—don't be intimidated, it only has four strings! You can be playing your first song in a day.✳

At the end of *The Lord of the Rings*, after the Ring has been destroyed, Sam and Frodo are brought before Aragorn✳ and his host of warriors and praised for their deeds. Sam is overwhelmed when a minstrel comes forward to sing the lay of "Frodo of the Nine Fingers and the Ring of Doom." Sam can't help but burst into tears. He and Frodo (and their adventure)

✳ The legendary rock trio Rush recorded a song titled "Rivendell" on their album *Fly by Night* in 1975.

✳ Viggo Mortensen (Aragorn from the film trilogy) came up with the haunting tunes for the song his character sings in the Elven-tongue when he is crowned King.

have *become* a song—a lay that will live on and inspire others long after they are gone from Middle-earth.

the wisdom of the shire tells us . . .

"Your voice wants to sing the story of your life. Let it be."

Chapter 17

THE ISTARI PROTOCOL

From the moment of Gandalf's creation by the Valar he has appeared in the body of an ordinary old man, stooped and wrinkled with a grey beard. He's the template for a wise counselor—a trustworthy mentor. As soon as he arrives at the Grey Havens he immediately sets out exploring Middle-earth as a self-described "stone doomed to rolling."＊

He becomes a helper to all of the good peoples of the lands, studying their histories and lore, while also traveling in disguise to distant countries, spying on the sinister inhabitants of Middle-earth. Gandalf visits the Shire from time to time, however, simply to relax. (Even though he's

＊ The Valar sent five Istari to Middle-earth, including Saruman the White, Gandalf the Grey, and Radagast the Brown. The names of the other two are unknown.

an Istari he has the body and needs of a human.) For centuries he's been hanging out, off and on, in the land of the Halflings, studying the curious little people called Hobbits.✳

✳ When Bilbo was born in the Shire, Gandalf had already lived in Middle-earth for 1,840 years.

✳ Old Toby's Leaf: tobacco or "pipe weed" as it's called in the Shire. In Gondor it's referred to as Westmansweed, and sweet galenas by the Rangers of the North.

Like them he enjoys tea-time and good ale and probably knows more about the family histories of the Bankses, Burrowses and Bagginses than they do. He's also taken up the curious habit, or "art" as the Hobbits call it, of smoking Old Toby's Leaf.✳ The wizard has become so enamored of the Shire he's gone a little native.

What is it about Hobbits that are so appealing to Gandalf? As he says to Frodo concerning Hobbits, "You can learn everything about them in a month, but after a hundred years they can still surprise you in a pinch." The Shire-folk are small, but they have huge hearts. They're good-natured, indomitable and quick-witted. And they never cheat at games (a point Frodo reminds Gandalf of with pride). Not only does Gandalf want to preserve this unique place from the coming wrath of Sauron, he senses the inhabitants of the Shire will be integral in some way in defeating that dark power.

When Bilbo meets Gandalf outside his front door at the start of *The Hobbit* he sees the wizard as a sort of

* Gandalf's various names were
The Grey Pilgrim, Mithrandir,
Stormcrow, and Tharkûn.
cheap conjuror—one step above, say, a traveling button salesman or a Sackville-Baggins. Gandalf is known for his wonderful fireworks, of course, but he seems a little shady to Bilbo. Not quite respectable. But that's all part of Gandalf's modus operandi. If he told people who and what he really was, they would be either terrified of him or think he was crazy. He hides his power and his keen intelligence so he can fit in and observe without drawing too much attention to himself.*

Cloaking oneself in modesty is a rare thing in our day and age, when people are encouraged to be as brash and outrageous as possible. It seems like the only people who do succeed are the ones who preen and blow their own horns the loudest. (The Internet, sadly, affords too many people this opportunity.) Politicians brag and boast about what they've done or say they'll do in a never-ending quest to substantiate their existence. For an Istari like Gandalf, the proof is in the pudding: your actions are all that count.

Even though Gandalf is filled with a hidden might (which becomes more prominent after his resurrection as Gandalf the White) the wizard does not dare to wield the One Ring. He knows that if he attempts to use Sauron's tool for good the very nature of the evil Ring will ultimately corrupt his righteous intentions and make him just as evil as Sauron. The One Ring is like a nuclear bomb. It has great power—but only the power to destroy.

Knowing your own limits is a concept that is not taught very often. We're told to push ourselves at all costs in a victory-or-nothing society. Winner takes all. Pull yourself up by your bootstraps. These are the hubristic apparitions of a trickle-down world. Gandalf might be a cranky old coot sometimes (especially with Peregrin Took) but he does not suffer from an ounce of hubris. Saruman and Sauron possess this flawed character trait of overweening pride, and it is the downfall of them both. Hobbits are the ultimate underdogs, the "little guy," and neither one of the villains sees them coming before it's too late.

Because Gandalf understands he cannot defeat Sauron alone he enlists everyone he can to be on his ragtag team—Hobbit gardeners, churlish Dwarves, talking trees, and a throne-less wandering king with a broken sword. A good leader sees talents in people who might have been overlooked because of some minor defect. That same leader respects and nurtures those talents, building up confidence instead of tearing it down.*

* Círdan the shipwright was the owner of the third Elven Ring of Power called Narya. But when Gandalf the Istari arrived in Middle-earth, Círdan gave him his "Ring of Fire," knowing the wizard would need all the extra help he could get in his fight against Sauron.

Rather than serving as an instigator of the action, Gandalf is the archetypal messenger or guide who sets the inhabitants of Middle-earth on their various paths, and reappears at crucial times in their adventures to either steer them in the right direction, or literally pull them from the fire. He's like a grumpy yet benevolent grandfather, especially to the Hobbits who, for their part, are Gandalf's unruly grandchildren.

At certain points Gandalf purposefully leaves the Shire-folk to their own devices so that they can grow and learn on their own. In *The Hobbit* he sends Bilbo and the Dwarves into the dread forest of Mirkwood alone (much to the ire of Thorin and the dejection of Bilbo). Gandalf warns them to stay on the path no matter what. Failing to heed his warning will most likely result in their untimely deaths. Of course they don't listen to him, and Bilbo is forced to find an inner strength he did not know he possessed to save his companions on more than one occasion.

Those of us who are parents know the precarious nature of trying to teach our children the dangers of the world, yet give them enough slack to make their own way. You can only warn an adventurous seven-year-old boy so many times that pogo-sticking on a snow-covered stairway at night is a bad idea. Sometimes you just have to let them take their lumps and learn the hard way.

Gandalf is more than just a father figure to the Hobbits, however. He's almost like a guru or spiritual teacher:

the Merlin or Obi-Wan Kenobi of Middle-earth. *The Lord of the Rings* had a huge resurgence of popularity during the late sixties and early seventies, when famous counterculture icons like The Beatles (Tolkien fans themselves)

* Gandalf befriended Aragorn when the Ranger was only twenty-five. Soon after Aragorn took on the assumed name Thorongil (presumably at Gandalf's behest) and spent the next twenty-three years as a Rider of Rohan, and as a man-at-arms for the city of Minas Tirith.

went looking for their own Gandalf in the guise of the Maharishi of India. The notion of a wise old man dispensing wisdom has been in the collective unconscious for thousands of years.*

At the beginning of *The Fellowship of the Ring*, when Frodo whines to Gandalf that he wishes Sauron's power had not grown during his lifetime, the wizard replies: "All we have to do is decide what to do with the time that is given us." We can't complain about our lot in life, Gandalf is saying. We need to have intention and then follow through with that intention. What's more, he's telling Frodo that we cannot control what has already happened in the past; we can only decide how we react in the moment. He's essentially giving Frodo the advice "Be here now," a tenent of Eastern mysticism filtered into the West.

Gandalf the Istari is mystical but he is not a mystic. He is not seeking disciples or attempting to start a little cult following in the Shire. He wants the Hobbits to come to the realization they can accomplish anything by their own devices. He is a servant of a higher power and seeks out mavericks like Aragorn the Ranger and Faramir of Gondor to be his friends. And who could be more of a freethinker than his boon companion throughout much of the story? None other than that rapscallion Peregrin "Pippin" Took.

One of Gandalf's best traits is his ability to take a punch and bounce back. When Pippin (the most interminably inquisitive Hobbit in the Shire) steals the *palantir* from a sleeping Gandalf and comes face-to-face with the horror of the burning eye of Sauron, the wizard knows he must leave for Minas Tirith immediately and take the Hobbit with him. The game has changed and so Gandalf must change with it. And the brief but potent message Gandalf shouts the moment before he slips into the abyss of Moria is ripe with meaning for us all: "Fly, you fools!" Don't just stand there gaping like an idiot when something goes amiss. Retreat, regroup, and live to fight again.

Gandalf isn't just a wise man. He is filled with compassion. Before the action of *The Lord of the Rings* begins Gandalf interrogates Gollum (after the wretch has been captured by Aragorn). But instead of killing the deceitful creature he stays his hand. He feels sorry for the horrid miserable thing, he later tells Frodo, because Gollum has been corrupted by the ultimate power of the Ring. He believes Gollum might have a part yet to play in the defeat of Sauron, and his instinct turns out to be right.

Gandalf must also use his reasoning skills when dealing with the emotional and temperamental inhabitants of Middle-earth. When he meets Théoden—the King of the Rohirrim—whose mind has been poisoned by his servant Wormtongue (turning the once valiant man into a near-paralytic heap of despair), Gandalf-the-psychologist essentially talks the morose Rider of Rohan through his angst with the aplomb of a seasoned depression counselor.

He leads Théoden to a window and enjoins him to look upon the beautiful fields of his homeland, to a place where the storm clouds are pulling back to reveal a shaft of brilliant light. The scales start to fall from Théoden's eyes. Gandalf tells the King he'd feel stronger with a sword in his hand rather than a staff, and Théoden suddenly agrees. The King of the Golden Hall never looks back, and rides to glory (albeit a glorious *death*).

On the surface this scene as it plays out in the book might not be as exciting as the film version, where Gandalf uses his staff to blast the demonic presence of Saruman from a possessed Théoden. But I think Tolkien's version is far more compelling. This Istari doesn't always have to fall back on magic to achieve his ends. Human insight mingled with the power to persuade is a valuable tool, and is often cast aside for more brutish or bombastic arguments in our own public debates.

Of course none of Gandalf's interpersonal skills can be used to persuade Denethor, the last Steward of Gondor, from his own staggering malaise. Denethor, suicidally depressed after the death of his favorite son, Boromir (and entrapped by his secret *palantir* that will only show him visions of horror and Sauron's impending triumph), is the quintessence of a leader who has lost faith in his own people. He covets the One Ring for himself, hoping to use it against Sauron in a last ditch effort.

The only hope for Gondor is Denethor's other son, Faramir. Fortunately, the gallant and shrewd Faramir studied with Gandalf in his youth, and wisely lets Frodo and Sam go after he has them—and the Ring—in his grasp. Mithrandir, as Gandalf is known in Gondor, must have impressed upon the young Faramir the perilous nature of attempting to wield an evil power in the name of virtue.

Even the wizard Saruman, an Istari like Gandalf, is not immune from the lust for power. He too hungers after the Ring, despite the fact that he knows he was sent to Middle-earth to watch over and counsel its inhabitants, rather than corrupting and dominating them. When Gandalf is brought back to life by the Valar after his fight to the death with the fire-whip-wielding Balrog, he is cloaked in white, a symbol of his purity—he has become what Saruman should have been.*

It would be wonderful if the leaders and mentors of our world had an inkling of Gandalf's incorruptibility, wouldn't it? The more power Gandalf gains throughout *The Lord of the Rings*, the more indestructible become his virtues. And, as Pippin says, this new white-robed version of Gandalf actually laughs more often than the old Gandalf. As his strength increases so does his humanity, which is usually the opposite of what happens in our world with powerful leaders.

One of the most important pieces of advice the wizard gives in *The Lord of the Rings* is something he says to Frodo back at Bag End at the start of the epic. He tells the scared Hobbit that he doesn't know why Frodo has been chosen to bear the burden of the Ring, but the Hobbit's only choice now is to carry through his task with "heart, courage and wit." Frodo and his friends do indeed help win the War of the Ring with these three traits, and they do it without losing their sense of what made them Hobbits—their humanity.

That is the Istari Protocol.

* Gandalf killed the Balrog (a creation of Morgoth) on the top of Zirakzigil—one of the peaks of Moria. The wizard died and was brought back to life by the Valar. The King of eagles carried him to Lothlórien where Galadriel clothed him in white.

* Ian McKellen, the awe-inspiring actor who plays Gandalf, is co-owner of a three-hundred-year-old pub called "The Grapes," at 76 Narrow Street, Limehouse, London. Sometimes he works there pulling pints. (thegrapes.co.uk)

At the end of *The Return of the King*, when Frodo, Sam, Merry and Pippin are riding back home with Gandalf, the wizard stops his horse near the border of the Shire. He tells the reluctant Hobbits they must return home without him. The Hobbits don't understand. They can't bear the idea of parting from their dear friend. The wizard informs them he has taught them all he can. They are "grown up" now, he says, and they're ready for anything the world outside the Shire might throw at them.*

the wisdom of the shire tells us . . .

"If you have been chosen for a particular and challenging task, face it with heart, courage and wit, and never lose sight of your compassion."

Chapter 18

BEARING THE BURDEN
OF YOUR RING

Imagine there are two magic rings of invisibility. One is given to a just person, the other to an unjust person. Both people can now sneak into stores and take whatever they want. Or creep into a bank or jewelry store and heist everything. They can kill with impunity, or ravish at will. They have become godlike. Would the just person be able to withstand this kind of temptation?

The Greek philosopher Plato didn't think so. He proposed an argument very similar to this one 2,400 years ago in his *Republic*. The magic ring in his discourse was modeled on the legend of Gyges, a shepherd who discovers a golden ring in a tomb that gives him the remarkable power to vanish.*

---

* *Yvain*, or *The Knight with the Lion*, was a twelfth-century French romance featuring a magic ring of invisibility.

Gyges uses his newfound source of power to seduce a queen, kill a king and take over a kingdom. Plato argued that members of a society believe (at least behind closed doors) that unjust behavior is more profitable than acting according to laws. His own society, he considered, would think a man a fool if he didn't use the power of a ring of invisibility to get what he wanted. (Does this kind of rationale remind anyone of a recent banking crisis?)

Tolkien certainly knew of the story of Gyges from his early childhood—he loved the Greek myths. And he probably read Plato's *Republic* while still a schoolboy, most likely in ancient Greek. The legend of Gyges and Plato's discourse on the ring of invisibility have echoes throughout Tolkien's stories. Gollum and Bilbo are the opposite sides of a coin—the just and unjust man who are both given the power of a ring of invisibility. Gollum uses it to murder babies in their sleep. Bilbo uses it to hide from those pesky Sackville-Bagginses. That's a big difference.*

Tolkien took this idea of a magic ring with corrupting powers and added a Norse twist. The story of a wizard or warlock depositing part of their spirit in an object outside of their body to keep it safe from harm is a common story in northern European mythology. A piece of Sauron's external soul is contained in the One Ring and it's made of a nearly imperishable

---

* The rumors of Gollum's atrocities were related by Gandalf to Frodo at Bag End in the chapter "The Shadow of the Past."

substance that can only be destroyed by melting it in the fires in which it was created. So long as the Ring still exists in Middle-earth, no matter if it's on the bottom of a river, or in the waistcoat pocket of a Hobbit in the Shire, Sauron's lingering spirit can find it one day and become whole again.*

* To amplify the power of the One Ring, Sauron had to place a great part of his soul into the nefarious tool. There were twenty Rings of Power including the One Ring.

* Isildur, the valiant hero of the previous age, who helped found Gondor and cut the Ruling Ring from Sauron's finger, knew the Ring was perilous when he wrote: "It is precious to me, though it causes me great pain."

Tolkien did not like people assigning allegories to his Ring of Doom. He even wrote how much he disliked "allegory in all its manifestations" in his foreword to a later edition of *The Lord of the Rings*. To him the Ring was what it was—an external-soul repository for a magical evil entity that has the power to corrupt all those who take possession of it (Isildur, Gollum, and eventually even Bilbo and Frodo). The spirit of the Ring is inherently destructive because Sauron's spirit has an insatiable lust for power and dominion over other living beings. Therefore the One Ring magnifies whatever bad traits are already inside the wearer of the Ring.*

For the rest of us, however, Sauron's Ring serves as a convenient analogy. It has seeped into the cultural subconscious: we all carry our own Ring of Doom. It could be some traumatic burden from the past, or a financial or health concern in the here and now. And most of us fear the future and the unknown, aka death. Whatever the case, the burden of our Ring will eventually destroy us, unless we let it go.

One of Frodo's greatest traits is his focus. Once he decides to accept the quest to destroy the Ring, he will not give up. He heads into Mordor understanding that he will never make it back home to his beloved Shire. His focus carries over to Sam who takes up the burden of the Ring when Frodo is captured by Orcs. Sam and Frodo go through terrible trials in Mordor, facing their worst fears. They overcome these challenges through sheer strength of will and the enduring power of true friendship—an example we can use in our relationships with our own friends.

I've seen the power of friendship to save someone burdened by a Ring of Doom. A dear childhood friend had become lost in despair and was drinking himself to death. His coworkers cared about him so much they held an intervention. My friend got into a program that involved climbing mountains with other addicts, and even though it was the challenge of his life, with every peak he summited his spirit was healed a little more. Everything changed about him for the better—his health, his looks, his sense of humor. He had rediscovered the joy of being alive: the pure joy of standing on the top of a fourteen-thousand-foot-tall mountain and knowing he was free.

The alternative to letting go of your burden is to end up like the depraved Gol-

✳ Gandalf realized Bilbo had become enslaved to the Ring when the Hobbit called it "precious," just like Isildur and Gollum had done before him.

lum, obsessed like some addict for a fix of the Ring. Even Bilbo, the kindhearted decent Hobbit obsessed with comfy armchairs and teatime is eventually consumed by the negative power of the Ring. Gandalf has to do his own little intervention at Bag End when he forces Bilbo to part with his treasure, handing the burden off to Frodo.✳

For his part, Frodo nearly has his soul ripped from his body in his effort to get the Ring to Mount Doom. By the end of the journey all of his memories of good things have been stripped from his being. He can't remember what food tastes like, or the feel of water or grass on his feet. He's consumed by the image of Sauron's "wheel of fire." And finally, when he's standing at the very Crack of Doom, he can't give up the Ring. He slips it on his finger, intending to keep it forever. His merciful treatment of Gollum—a creature even more consumed by his lust for the precious object than Frodo—is the only thing that saves the Hobbit from failing in his quest and becoming yet another Gollum.

The gentle gardener Samwise Gamgee is also not immune to the power of the Ring to create delusions of grandeur in the one who possesses it. Sam takes the Ring after

* In Sam's fantasy he was called "Samwise the Strong, Hero of the Age," and wielded a flaming sword.

Frodo is poisoned by She-lob with the intention of keeping it from falling into the hands of the enemy.

Soon after the Ring starts to create "wild fantasies" in the modest Hobbit's mind. He imagines himself as some kind of Middle-earth superhero, marching at the head of a great army to attack Sauron's realm. He sees himself wielding godlike powers, bringing the wastes of Mordor back to life with a mere sweep of his hand. But then his "plain Hobbit-sense" takes control. He comprehends a simple truth: he does not have the strength to carry such a burden. All he really needs in life, he knows in his heart, is to be a free man, with his own little garden.*

The wisdom of the Shire is in Sam's bones.

Those of us who dwell outside the Shire find it more difficult to let go of our yearning for power and approbation. And we humans are prodigiously opportunistic about it. How else can you explain the phenomenon of candidates seeking high-level positions in government for which they are absolutely unqualified, or talentless nitwits parading their inane lives on TV and the Internet and accepting the title of "stars"?

I've had my own taste of delusion. When I was a teenager I won a prestigious playwriting contest and had my work produced off-Broadway. I grew up in a small town, two blocks away from the actor Kyle MacLachlan (whose movie *Blue Velvet* had just come out), and I assumed people from our neighborhood must be destined for fame. After my play opened to critical acclaim I was approached by the legendary publishers Samuel French to print my work. I left their office one golden September day, my first writing contract clutched in my hand, and felt like I owned New York City—Arthur Miller watch out! As I walked blithely down the sidewalk on Forty-fifth Street, practicing my Tony Award speech, a homeless man stumbled blindly into my path from an alley. He latched onto me—grabbed me by both arms and breathed his boozy breath into my face saying, "Hey kid. Can you spare some money? I'm a *playwright* down on his luck."

I suppose I should have bought him a sandwich and asked him what had gone wrong with his career. I might have learned a valuable lesson about life in the theater. But I didn't. Instead, I took off running in terror as if I'd seen the Ghost of Future Failed Playwrights. I never had another play produced after that initial success. No matter how hard I tried. My failure as a playwright haunted me for years and soured my life and career, and I often thought of that poor Gollum-like wretch who prophesied my doom as a thespian. I eventually found fulfillment as a writer and a creative person in many different ways. But as a playwright? Nope. One day I finally tossed aside that desire—like an evil ring into a lava pit—and watched it melt away.

* Boromir rode 110 days from Gondor to Rivendell, all alone on dangerous paths, to seek Elrond's advice. This was no small feat in the Third Age.

Sometimes the Ring of Doom is somebody else's burden that carries over to your own life. Boromir was a valiant man and virtuous of heart. In any other tale he would have been one of the heroes of the story.* But Boromir's father was Denethor, a Man corrupted by an insane hunger to seize the Ring and use it for himself. Denethor infuses Boromir with this heavy charge—to bring the Ring to Gondor no matter what the cost. The price for Boromir is the loss of his honor when he tries to take the Ring from Frodo. He knows in his heart the Ring is evil, but "a madness" overtakes his soul—and the longing to make his father proud.

Just because somebody we know or love has an obsession or a bad habit doesn't mean we have to let it taint our lives. Your life is your own and shouldn't be an extension of somebody else's aspirations or a reflection of their foibles. We have the power to focus our thoughts in a positive way and to decide how to best use the time we have. The way you do that is by making a concerted effort to rein in negative desires and magnify the beneficial ones.

The Shire-folk are more fortunate than us. Our modern lives are so incredibly complicated and fraught with anxiety compared to theirs. The Hobbits set about fixing an unfavorable situation or a bad state of mind with a practical solution. If you were a Hobbit and complaining of being overweight, one of your friends would hand you a walking stick and say with a smile, "Let's go for a long stroll toward Woody End." If you hated your job at the mill at Bywater, working for that good-for-nothing Ted Sandyman, someone might suggest you start your own mill up the river. It's a free Shire, right? Down in the dumps? Get to work in your garden—because it's full of weeds! Can't sleep at night? You need more walking and gardening. Sick at heart? Seek out your friends and tell them your woes. Magic Ring of Doom burning a hole in your velvet waistcoat pocket?

Go ahead and melt it.

the wisdom of the shire tells us . . .

"Bear your own Ring of Doom only for as long as you deem necessary. When the time is right, cast it into the fire and be free of the burden."

Chapter 19

THE LIGHT OF EÄRENDIL

In *The Fellowship of the Ring* Galadriel gives Frodo a special gift before he departs the sacred woods of Lothlórien. It's a crystal phial containing the light of a star called "Eärendil." Frodo and Sam use this magical light several times in their journey through Mordor, saving themselves from danger in the darkest depths of Sauron's demonic realm.

Eärendil was a mortal Man of the First Age of Middle-earth, the period taking place over ten thousand years before the action of *The Lord of the Rings*, which Tolkien wrote about in his post-humously published saga *The Silmarillion*.✳ Eärendil was a bold mariner who sailed to the Undy-

✳ Silmaril: one of the three mystical jewels fashioned by the Elf Fëanor. They held supernatural light of the Two Trees of Valinor and were stolen by Morgoth and taken to Middle-earth where he set them in an iron crown.

ing Lands with one of the famed Silmaril jewels affixed to his helm—to beg the help of the Valar in fighting Morgoth (the fallen Valar and master of the young Sauron). The Queen of the Stars eventually placed Eärendil in the firmament—turned him into a heavenly body so the light of the surviving Silmaril could shine as a beacon for all of Middle-earth.＊

> ＊ The Valar were so moved by Eärendil's plea that they agreed to help the people of Middle-earth and sent an army to attack Morgoth. He was captured and his spirit cast out beyond the boundaries of creation.
>
> ＊ Other heavenly bodies in Middle-earth were "The Plow" (the Big Dipper) and the red star "Borgil" (Betelgeuse).

The "star" of Eärendil is actually our planet Venus—the brightest object in our sky after the sun and moon. It's been a part of our own world's mythology for thousands of years, just like it was for the Hobbits and the other inhabitants of Middle-earth. Like Venus, Eärendil is so bright it can actually cast a shadow at night. And based on the position of its orbit around the sun it can change from the evening star to the morning star.＊

The mythos of Eärendil is contained in Tolkien's very first writings about Middle-earth, penned nearly a hundred years ago. The story of this Man who became a star is the seed from which grew all of Tolkien's universe and it was created during a time of great anxiety for the author while he was finishing his university studies, knowing he

* Trench fever is caused by body lice. The symptoms include a high fever, aching eyeballs, and leg pain. Two other famous writers—A.A. Milne and C.S. Lewis—were also hospitalized for this disease during WWI.

* Mythopoeia: from the Greek, meaning "fable-making."

would have to go to war as soon as he was done. The slaughter of the trenches loomed ahead, and so he found relief in a fantasy world of his own creation. He would begin to work in earnest on the mythology of Middle-earth while recovering from trench fever in an army hospital after being discharged from combat.*

For such a devout Catholic and true believer in the Christian faith, Tolkien used a remarkable amount of restraint in keeping his own religious beliefs out of Middle-earth. There is not a single mention of the word "God" in either *The Hobbit* or *The Lord of the Rings*. It's one of the reasons the stories are so popular around the world—despite the complex mythopoeia Tolkien didn't try to impose a theology upon the reader.*

There are godlike creatures in Tolkien's mythology, however. They are called the Valar, the angelic children of the one god Ilúvatar. The Valar are blessed with the gift of subcreation—they can bring to life their own creatures to inhabit Middle-earth. The Elves, Ents, Dwarves and Men and even the Hobbits are all "invented" by the Valar who are like a team of wild video game designers populating *World of Warcraft*.

The light of Eärendil is also a symbol of insight. When Galadriel takes Frodo to her mirror of prophecy, they stand under the light of the evening star shining brightly above—shining so brightly the star casts her shadow on the ground. Suddenly, Frodo sees a ring on her finger, glittering brightly as if the Star of Eärendil "had come down to rest upon her hand." It's only then Frodo realizes Galadriel is wearing one of the three rings Sauron made for the Elves. Galadriel explains that the destruction of the One Ring—to which the Elven rings are bound—will cause the decline of Elven power in Middle-earth.

Impulsively, Frodo holds out the Ring for her to take it. Galadriel is tempted by his offer of the "Great Ring" as she calls it. In one of Tolkien's most powerful monologues she imagines herself the master of the Ring, with the people of Middle-earth falling before her in "love and despair" like some sort of terrible goddess. Galadriel quickly realizes this choice could only lead to disaster, and understands the Valar have sent a final test of her character. With the Star of Eärendil shining over her head, and lighting up her countenance in the reflection of her glowing ring, the Elven Queen is literally illuminated by the wisdom of Eärendil. She releases her desire for ultimate power and accepts that she must now follow a new path.

Why is enlightenment so difficult to find in our own lives? Many of us set out determinedly on quests for self-knowledge, only to end up more confused than when we

* The other two sayings at the
Oracle at Delphi were "Make a
vow and mischief will come
your way," and "Nothing in
excess."

began. Or perhaps we find
someone we think can teach
us important truths, only
to discover they have some
self-serving agenda. Often
those who seek enlightenment are mocked by a world that
values nothing more than wealth and power.

Over the door to the Temple of Delphi in ancient
Greece was carved the saying "Know thyself."* Introspec-
tion was an important notion to the Athenians. They felt
they did, in fact, know themselves. For a while they were
masters of their world and made groundbreaking discov-
eries in the disciplines of art and science. But then the
Athenians plunged their society into a meaningless war
with their rival Sparta, ruining their "Golden Age" and
destroying their independence for over two thousand
years.

Do you feel like you really know yourself and your
place in the society in which you live? Or are you buffeted
about like a boat on a stormy sea? Pulled hither and thither,
chasing after something (or somebody) that you don't really want or need? The real question is, "What makes you
truly happy?" And can you gain this happiness without
creating more problems for yourself and everyone around
you? What if we placed a higher value on quality of life
rather than outward success, and tried to make this happen
by simplifying everything in our lives? It's a counterintui-

tive notion, but one the Shire-folk understand. "Getting and spending, we lay waste our powers," as the poet Wordsworth so wisely wrote ninety years before Tolkien was born.

The phial Galadriel gives to Frodo is an extremely supernatural object. It's a crystal container filled with the water from her sacred mirror—water that has been saturated with the mystical light of the Star of Eärendil. Frodo and Sam discover the light can be activated by uttering certain phrases in the Elven-tongue: words that spring magically from their mouths. The phial, supercharged with these incantations, glows to life, warding off Shelob, terrifying Orcs, and breaking the paralyzing spell wrought by the stone Watchers at the gates of Cirith Ungol.

At their darkest moment in Mordor—on the barren plains of Gorgoroth—with their journey seemingly going on forever like an "ever-darkening dream," Sam and Frodo escape into hallucinations, imagining they're back in sunny Hobbiton. In this wasted land, with Mount Doom billowing black smoke into the sky, even the stars are blotted out at night. Sam never lets go of the phial of Galadriel, however. He wears it around his neck—a glowing symbol of goodness and hope, the antithesis to the evil Ring of Doom on its golden necklace, weighing down Frodo's head like a millstone.

When Sam and Frodo are approaching Mount Doom, and everything seems miserable and hopeless, Sam sees the black clouds of Mordor part to reveal a single star shining in the night. "The beauty of it smote his heart," and suddenly, Sam is filled with hope, just from the sight of this single star.

Years ago I was co-executive producer of a film about the looting of archeological sites in Iraq post–U.S. invasion. The filmmaker behind the project, a man named Micah, was kidnapped by insurgents who threatened to execute him. When I got the call from his fiancée telling me what had happened, it felt like someone had stabbed me in the gut. I've never felt so sick and helpless in my life. Many nights during this ordeal I stood outside alone looking up at the stars, wondering how this colleague—a brave, decent and passionate man—could end up in this hell. Usually the vastness of the night sky made me feel insignificant. But during this time the stars seemed to connect me to everyone else out there who was hoping and praying for Micah's release.

All of us would benefit from our own phial of Galadriel—some magical bottled starlight that could shine out in the dark times of our lives. Life can be exhausting, terrifying and heartbreaking. Anyone who's lost a loved one, or suffered an injury or illness, or been let go from a job knows the profound despair that seems to blot out the sun and the stars and turn the whole world to a never-ending gloom, a nightmare that won't end.

I've experienced my own share of losses and trials and

setbacks, and each one of these challenges has led me on its own grim and twisting path fraught with pain and frustration. But "Where there's life, there's hope," as the Old Gaffer says. You just have to keep on keepin' on until, eventually, you fight your way out of the dark.

Micah, the documentary filmmaker, was let go after ten days in captivity. We'll never know for sure why the insurgents released him. Perhaps it was the plea his fiancée and sister made begging the kidnappers for mercy. Maybe it was the influence of Islamic clerics who'd been told about Micah's altruistic work in Iraq. Whatever the case, he was set free, and that day was one of the happiest of my life. Neither his life nor the people who cared about him would ever be the same again.

Back home at Bag End after the War of the Ring, Frodo tries to settle back into his old uncomplicated life in the Shire. It's not the same for the Ring-bearer anymore, though. He saved the Shire but not for himself. He watches happily as Sam gets married and sets up house with Rosie Cotton, and even helps name their firstborn child.*

Sadly, Frodo can never recover from his many injuries. He's been stabbed by a Morgul-blade, poisoned by a giant spider, beaten by Orcs and tortured by the agony of bearing the Ring. His tormented soul can only be healed by going to the source of all life in

---

* Elanor, Sam and Rosie's firstborn child, was named for the white flowers that grew in Lothlórien.

*The enigmatic craftsman who built their ship—an ancient Elf named Círdan—is the same shipwright who helped make the sailor Eärendil's boat eons before.

Middle-earth—to Valinor. The role he played in destroying the evil of Sauron has earned him this rare passage to the home of the gods.

Frodo completes his tale of the War of the Ring, and gives *The Red Book of Westmarch* to Sam who is now the master of Bag End. The Ring-bearer sets out for the Grey Havens (the Elven port a hundred and fifty miles to the west of the Shire) on his favorite horse, named "Strider" in honor of his friend who is now known as King Elessar. Here Frodo boards a white ship for the Undying Lands alongside Gandalf, Galadriel, Elrond and Bilbo.*

Sam, Merry and Pippin watch the boat slowly disappear into the grey mist of the inlet. Frodo is standing at the stern of the ship, and he holds up the phial of Galadriel for his friends on shore to see one last time. A final glimmer emanates from the crystal decanter: the light of Eärendil—a symbol of enduring hope, determination and wisdom that will never fade.

The three friends ride back home to the Shire with tears in their eyes and Gandalf's last words in their thoughts—"Go in peace! I will not say: do not weep; for not all tears are an evil." They will miss their beloved friends Frodo, Bilbo and their wizard mentor. But the goodness of the Shire-folk will endure, and they will continue to enjoy the simple but wonderful pleasures of their country: food, friends, gardening, warm hearth-fires and cozy armchairs, the laughter of children, a good mug of ale, long walks and the beauty of trees, presents and parties and, most important of all, peace.*

* Legolas constructed his own ship to sail to the Undying Lands and was the last of the Companions to leave Middle-earth along with a single passenger—his dear friend Gimli, probably clutching three strands of golden hair encased in crystal on a chain round his neck.

the wisdom of the shire tells us . . .

"May the light of Eärendil glow for you as a steadfast beacon of hope and insight, glittering in the dawn and dusk of your life."

Chapter 20

THE FOURTH AGE

After Aragorn is crowned King he asks his mentor Gandalf if he will stay in Gondor to council him during his reign. The wizard, however, has already booked himself passage on a one-way trip to Valinor. He tells Aragorn that the Third Age—which had been Gandalf's epoch in Middle-earth—has ended, and the Fourth Age has begun. It's now the Age of Men.

We are living in our own Fourth Age. Humankind dominates the planet, there's no doubt about that. We've been so busy producing and consuming we've actually altered our climate. Some scientists refer to the last two hundred years (since the start of the Industrial Revolution) as the Anthropocene period. The word means the era of the "new man." In this short span of time humans have significantly altered biodiversity on our planet for the worse.

This is also the Age of Technology, and our various gadgets fascinate us and govern our lives in so many ways. The mobile device is our new magic. But what about the old magic? The splendor of the natural world and the miracle of living? Is this kind of enchantment eventually going to vanish from the Earth? Are facsimiles of life, such as massively multiplayer online games, really better than the massive multiplicity of *real* life? Do you want to wear Google's glasses? Because I don't.

There are so many lessons to be learned from the Hobbits. But one of the most essential is the question of wants and needs. The Shire-folk *need* many things: food, friendship, fun, sleep, taking delight in nature and exercise just to name a few. Their *wants*, however, are scanty and utilitarian. They want the tools to do their work, a snug little home to call their own, and clothes to keep them warm.

It seems like we twenty-first-century people have so many wants we don't know what to do with ourselves. The wants rule out our needs and drive us to ruin our emotional and physical health in pursuit of that elusive dragon's hoard. And we forget about the truly important things that make us happy—the things that are as free as the air, like our relationships with friends, family and children. Are we really going to allow the credit card consortiums to burden us with crushing debt while they cheat at the game and grow more powerful and rapacious?

Sometimes it feels like the Sarumans and the Saurons of the world are winning, doesn't it? Where is an Elrond or Gandalf to guide us? Where's an Aragorn to lead us? The truth is we just can't wait for them anymore. We need to heed Merry's advice when he says the Hobbits will never take back the Shire by merely looking "shocked and sad" about the evil that's been done to their beloved home while they've been away. We have to take action, and that means participating in civic life, being a part of our communities, and not sitting by passively as powerful people or corporations do evil things to us and our environment.

Back in the '70s the slogan "Frodo Lives!" ✳became a symbol of the counterculture movement. It appeared on T-shirts, on graffiti in subway tunnels, and bumper stickers. In *The Lord of the Rings* Frodo's friends never gave up hope (no matter how bad things got) that the Hobbit would suc-

---

✳ "Many of those who first caught sight of 'Frodo Lives' in the subway, or scribbled on a billboard, didn't know who Frodo was, or John Ronald Reuel Tolkien, or Middle-earth itself, for that matter. *The Hobbit* and *The Lord of the Rings* were a kind of password to shared secret knowledge. People who already knew the books found their own meanings, went on their own interior quests; people who didn't were strangely lured, as though by the word *'mellon'*—the Elvish for 'friend.'"

—Peter S. Beagle, author of *The Last Unicorn* and the introduction to *The Lord of the Rings*

ceed in his seemingly impossible quest to Mount Doom to destroy the Ring. The message behind the "Frodo Lives!" catchphrase was the idea that the "little guy" could win any struggle.

The Shire isn't a real place. We all know that. But the standards of the Hobbits can be our own. Being a part of the Shire means believing in the concepts of egalitarianism and morality. A way of living that is sustainable and sufficient. It's about having a demeanor of good cheer and civility. Hobbits are totally present and aware of what's going on around them. They're so focused on life they really don't have time to ponder death. And they share a deep friendship with the earth.

The more people who believe in the Shire and what it stands for, the less likely it will slowly begin to fade from the world, leaving nothing behind but a story in a book. We love this place that Tolkien invented because we want to go there. As Peter S. Beagle wrote almost half a century ago in his essay "Tolkien's Magic Ring," "Something of ourselves has gone into reading it, and so it belongs to us."

The Shire can become as real as we make it in our own lives and communities and countries. It doesn't have to exist merely in our thoughts or on the tour of a movie set in New Zealand. There are millions of fans of Tolkien's books as well as Peter Jackson's film adaptations. Imagine what we might be able to accomplish if we raised our voices together in a fellowship of the Shire. We would be a force to be reckoned with. "The Shire lives!" could be the motto of our own Fourth Age.

We all have the potential to do extraordinary things just like a modest Hobbit, or even an unassuming professor of philology who wrote treasured classics that have stood the test of time. But first we have to start our journey on "the Road" as Bilbo called the adventure that is life. He likened this adventure to a great river with a source at each doorstep where "every path was its tributary."

Try opening your heart to new ways of doing things. Don't be afraid of the cynics and the Orcs of the world. The only thing holding you back is your own self-doubt and the burdens of the past that, hopefully, you are ready to let go of—like a cursed ring slipping from your finger. And then you will find yourself on one of those paths leading to the Road.

Our lives have great potential to be exciting adventures, and there are risks along the way, but they're definitely risks worth taking. If your feet are grounded in a system of beliefs that are as solid and enduring as those born in the Shire, you'll be certain to reach your goals at every stage along the Road of your long and happy life.

In the words of Aragorn, "May the Shire live for ever unwithered!"

the wisdom of the shire tells us . . .

"*All paths lead to the Road, and the wisdom will guide you there and back to the Shire—a country that exists inside our hearts, a truth that is revealed to the world by our honorable actions.*"

*

THE HOBBIT TEST

Are you a Hobbit? Or are you still on your way to Hobbiton? Perhaps, dear reader, you are actually just an Orc. Let the Hobbit Test begin. Mark an X in the box next to each statement that suits you and then tally up your points.

20 points each

☐ You're still hungry after second breakfast.

☐ You've called somebody an "Orc" in anger.

☐ You have more hair on your feet than your head.

☐ You feel that Dwarves are looked down upon.

☐ You've referred to a very boring person as being "Ent-like."

40 points each

☐ You think Neiman Marcus might carry *mithril*.

☐ You think drinking beer is a decent way to hydrate.

☐ You believe velvet waistcoats will make a comeback.

☐ You wonder if Halflings might really live in New Zealand.

☐ You don't like seeing Elijah Wood with facial hair.

60 points each

☐ You think iPhone's face-time should be called "*palantir*-time."

☐ You like plump Peter Jackson better than skinny Peter Jackson.

☐ You've named one of your cars after a Tolkien character.

☐ You know how many farthings there are in the Shire.

☐ You've walked barefoot in the snow for fun.

80 points each

☐ You've smoked a pipe and pretended you were a Hobbit.

☐ You admire Gandalf, but when Legolas draws an arrow, you quiver.

☐ You have hidden rare cheeses from your roommates in your fridge.

☐ You would like a bumper sticker that says, I BRAKE FOR OLIPHAUNTS.

☐ You've named one of your pets after a Tolkien character.

100 points each

☐ You've fought somebody over a mushroom appetizer.

☐ You think James Gandolfini has the coolest actor name.

☐ You know what J.R.R. stands for.

☐ You sometimes look at your gold wedding ring and whisper, "The precious."

☐ You've suggested Elladan and Elrohir as names for twins.

200 points each

☐ You think in Sindarin, but you dream in Quenya.

☐ You would consider a tattoo of Viggo as Strider on your posterior.

☐ You think you have the answer to the enigma that is Tom Bombadil.

☐ You own a Shadowfax CD.

☐ You've named one of your children after a Tolkien character.

Total _____

Scores

300 points or above: **Super Hobbit**

200 points or above: **A hard Hobbit to break**

100 points or above: **A genuine Hobbit**

70 points or above: **Definitely Hobbittish**

50 points or above: **On your way to Hobbiton**

0 points: **You are an Orc**

✳

DIRECTIONS FOR CREATING A
SMALL HOBBIT GARDEN

Let's assume that you have space for a 4' by 8' garden bed. You can plant a variety of vegetables and herbs in a space that small (see diagram). But seeds can be very expensive if you're only using a couple from each packet. A lot of people have come up with clever ways to get around this: they're sharing seeds.

Throw a "Seed Exchange Party" and invite everyone you know who is interested in having a garden. Guests bring a couple of packets of seeds, you put them on a big table and then you each take a few. Remember, you only need half a dozen cucumber seeds to grow enough cukes for an entire summer.

Craigslist and Freecycle are great places to look for free gardening material like old hoses (which can be repaired with inexpensive new hose ends), watering cans, tools, pots, plastic barrels for collecting rainwater and even lumber for building raised beds. Check out the website www.dirtcheapgardening.com for some awesome ideas on creating inexpensive (and sometimes free!) gardens.

You can also use your entire neighborhood as a garden. Lots of people have fruit trees but never even pick the harvest. You can offer to make baked goods or jam in return for taking their unwanted fruit. This is also a great way to meet your neighbors.

Cut off the sod where you want to plant your garden bed and shake out all the dirt and worms. Get four or five bags of compost to mix into the soil, along with some organic fertilizer (like cottonseed and kelp meal). I've used bat guano for nitrogen before and it works great. You don't have to dig deep down or spend hours churning the soil. Your seeds want to grow. All they need now is some sun and water.

Directions for laying out your bed for peas, tomatoes, carrots, lettuce, cucumbers and basil:

1. Lay out your bed in an east/west direction. Along the back of your bed put in two poles so they're at least 6' out of the ground, and stretch some jute at 8" intervals between them. Plant a row of sugar snap or snow peas so they grow up the jute creating a wall of

pea vines. This will be the first crop you sow and that's why you want it on the north side of the bed, otherwise it will screen off all the other plants from the sun.

2. Mix up some heirloom lettuce seeds (like flashy or bib) in the palm of your hand—about half a teaspoon's worth. Now pinch some between your fingers and sprinkle it in the designated lettuce patch. Once the seed has been cast, simply cover it with about half an inch of soil. Lettuce leaves can be pinched off all summer long rather than pulling the entire plant from the ground. They'll just grow new leaves for you to eat.

3. Plant your carrot seeds in shallow rows. You might want to mix in a little sand in this area to help the carrots push through the soil. Try Red or Purple Dragon varieties in honor of Smaug.

4. Buy a couple of tomato starts from your local farmers market such as Brandywine (maybe they came from Buckland!) or Purple Cherokee. Pinch off the first couple of branches near the root base and bury them so the dirt covers these pinched-off places. You might want to consider caging your tomatoes or

putting in a big wooden stake. They will grow up to 4' in height.

5. Make a small mound for the cucumbers and plant three seeds in the top. Once they sprout and have time to grow, pinch off the smallest one and let the two biggest plants grow. Try lemon cucumbers—they have a sweet taste and should be picked when they're about the size of a lemon. Armenian cucumbers are another interesting variety.

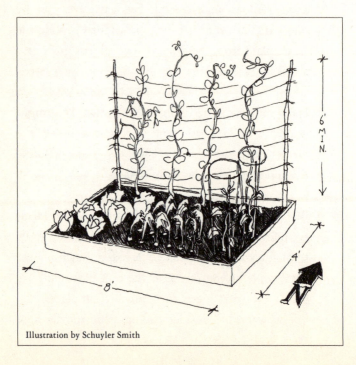

Illustration by Schuyler Smith

6. In late spring dig a shallow trough (half an inch deep) along the front of the bed and sprinkle in the basil seeds. Cover them with a thin layer of soil. You can also buy basil starts if you want them to grow faster. As soon as the top leaves are big enough you can pinch off the top of the plant (leaving the tiny new leaves below to grow). Basil, like lettuce, will create new leaves over and over again. Snip off any flowers that bloom to keep the leaves from getting bitter. At the end of the season pull the entire plant and make pesto by blending the leaves with olive oil and garlic.

7. In November, plant some garlic cloves in the back of the bed where the peas were. They need to grow all winter and can be harvested the following summer.

To attract bees early in the season and throughout the summer, plant some seeds of the flower called "Bee's Friend" (*Lacy Phacelia*). Butterflies love the purple flowers too.

Always remember to have patience and every season you'll learn something new to carry over to the next. Keep in mind the Old Gaffer's wise words of wisdom about gardening: "You live and learn."

ACKNOWLEDGMENTS

The Wisdom of the Shire would never have been published without the supreme efforts of my agent, Adam Chromy, and the faith and guidance of my editor, Peter Joseph, at Thomas Dunne Books.

I would also like to offer my gratitude to foreign rights maven Heather Baror-Shapiro; to my Hobbit uncles, Richard and Bart; to my childhood Tolkien brethren, Benjamin and Daniel Thompson; and to my encouraging friends David Wheeler, Murat Armbruster, and Peter S. Beagle.

Finally, an eternal thank you to my mom, Linda, and my wife, Kendra—my morning and evening stars.